DON'T DOUBT
IN THE DARK

DON'T DOUBT IN THE DARK

50 WAYS TO OVERCOME DOUBT WITH FAITH AND HOPE

GEORGE SWEETING

MOODY PRESS
CHICAGO

© 2000 by
GEORGE SWEETING

All Scripture quotations, unless otherwise indicated, are taken from the *Ryrie Study Bible, New King James Version* (Chicago: Moody, 1985). *The Holy Bible,* copyright © 1979, 1980, 1982 by Thomas Nelson, Inc. Used by permission. All rights reserved.

Scripture quotations marked (NASB) are taken from the *New American Standard Bible®.* Copyright © 1960, 1962, 1963, 1968, 1971, 1972, 1973, 1975, 1977, 1995 by The Lockman Foundation. Used by permission.

Scripture quotations marked (NIV) are taken from the *Holy Bible: New International Version®.* NIV®. Copyright © 1973, 1978, 1984 by International Bible Society. Used by permission of Zondervan Publishing House. All rights reserved.

The "NIV" and "New International Version" trademarks are registered in the United States Patent and Trademark Office by International Bible Society. Use of either trademark requires the permission of International Bible Society.

Scripture quotations marked (NLT) are taken from the *Holy Bible, New Living Translation,* copyright © 1996. Used by permission of Tyndale House Publishers, Inc., Wheaton, Illinois 60189. All rights reserved.

Scripture quotations marked (KJV) are taken from the King James Version.

Scripture quotations marked (TLB) are taken from *The Living Bible* © 1971. Used by permission of Tyndale House Publishers, Inc., Wheaton, IL. 60189.

Scripture quotations marked (AMPLIFIED) are taken from the *Amplified Bible* © 1965 by Zondervan Publishing House.

Library of Congress Cataloging-in-Publication Data

Sweeting, George, 1924-
Don't doubt in the dark : fifty ways to overcome doubt with faith and hope / George Sweeting.
p. cm.
Includes bibliographical references.
ISBN 0-8024-8334-8 (trade paper)
1. Christian life. 2. Belief and doubt. 3. Consolation. I. Title: Do not doubt in the dark.
II. title.

BV4501.2.S879 2000
234'.2--dc21

99-058004

1 3 5 7 9 10 8 6 4 2

Printed in the United States of America

This book is dedicated to the life and memory of my boyhood pastor,
Herrmann George Braunlin,
who was for me an unforgettable role model and beloved friend.

The dedication also includes his superb successor,
Pastor John Minnema,
and the faithful, gracious people of the Hawthorne Gospel Church.
They continue to be a part of my life.

Contents

Preface   9
1. Don't Doubt in the Dark   11
2. Pick Up the Pieces   15
3. Caravaggio's *Doubting Thomas*   19
4. A Supernatural Attitude   23
5. Eve—A Woman of Faith   27
6. My First Goals   31
7. Augustine's Transformation   35
8. Contrary Winds   39
9. The Man with the Ticking Heart   43
10. Success Depends on Your Choices   47
11. The Master Artist   51
12. Worried Sick   53
13. Jochebed—The Mother of Moses   57
14. This Hospital Bed . . . Is My Altar   61
15. The Chicago Fire Catastrophe   63
16. Don't Crowd Out Love   67
17. God Cares for You   71
18. Vincent Van Gogh—An Evangelist!   75
19. No One Drifts to Heaven   79
20. Try the Uplook   83

21. Bathsheba—The Power to Change 87
22. Be a Builder 91
23. Word Power 95
24. The Puzzle of Life 99
25. Esther—A Hero Forever 103
26. Created to Fly 107
27. The Virgin's Name Was Mary 111
28. C. H. Spurgeon's Glory and Grief 115
29. Love—Lost and Found 119
30. D. L. Moody's Rebellious Son 123
31. William James Sweeting . . . A.D. 1511 127
32. Turning on the Power 129
33. Only That Which Is Eternal . . . Matters 133
34. Thank You, Billy 137
35. You Can Be a Rope Holder 141
36. Joni Earickson Tada 145
37. How to Have a Happy Day 149
38. Henry Crowell of Quaker Oats 153
39. Humpty-Dumpty Was Pushed 159
40. Jonathan Edwards—A Master of Prose 163
41. My Angel Mother 167
42. God—God—Yes! 171
43. Wanted: Intercessors 175
44. The Thistle—Scotland's Emblem 179
45. Consider My Servant Job 181
46. He Who Laughs . . . Lasts 185
47. My Very Best Friend 189
48. Moody's Last Year of Faith 193
49. But Some Doubted 197
50. Anchors to Hold 199

"Don't Doubt
In the Dark"

C S. Lewis said, "God whispers to us in our pleasure, speaks to us in our conscience, but shouts to us in our pain."[1]

This book deals with the subject of doubting, sickness, and pain along with words of hope and faith. In the summer of 1950, I had the honor of meeting V. Raymond Edman, President of Wheaton College. Both of us were speakers at a conference in Schroon Lake, New York. Dr. Edman's life and ministry left a lasting mark upon me as well as thousands of others.

During that week, Dr. Edman shared two unforgettable phrases. He read a radio script given in 1937 by William Cameron of the Ford Motor Company titled "Too Soon to Quit." I chose this as the title of my last book. The complete phrase shared by President Edman was "It's always too soon to quit."

Another phrase used by Dr. Edman was "Don't doubt in the dark what God has revealed in the light." That's the theme of this series of essays.

I hope you will find inspiration and challenge in each chapter.

NOTE

1. C. S. Lewis, *The Problem of Pain* (New York: Macmillan, 1962), 93.

1

Don't Doubt
in the Dark

Don't doubt in the dark . . . what God has revealed in the light. And yet, we do doubt . . . as we struggle in the dark places of life.

One of my childhood heroes was John the Baptist. Everything about him intrigued me. He was a rugged, outdoor, nature-loving champion of the people. His clothing was made from camel's hair, he sported a leather belt, and his diet was wild honey and locusts. John was a "real man."

Jesus called John the greatest person who ever lived (see Matthew 11:11; Luke 7:28) . . . and that's impressive.

His popularity was so great that crowds—from Jerusalem, Judea, and the entire area—flocked to see and hear him.

John's life modeled humility (Luke 3:16), honesty (Matthew 3:7), and purity (Luke 1:15). His popularity was enormous.

However, one day he openly rebuked King Herod for taking his brother's wife, Herodias, as his live-in girlfriend. John pointed his gun-like finger at Herod and said, "It is not lawful for you to have your brother's wife" (Mark 6:18).

Herodias was furious and plotted revenge, resulting in John's arrest and imprisonment.

While languishing in jail, away from the crowds and the euphoria of success . . . John began to doubt. Though still in his thirties, his life hung by the thread of a crowd-pleasing king and his scheming mistress. John's doubt intensified in the darkness.

John's doubt grew so large that he sent two of his disciples to Jesus and asked, "Are You the Coming One, or do we look for another?" (Matthew 11:3).

If John, the greatest person who ever lived, doubted, then it's reasonable that we too should have our share of doubts.

How are we to cope with the hurts of life? Though there are no easy answers, we can follow John's example. John brought his doubts to Jesus.

Jesus told John's disciples, "Go and tell John the things which you hear and see: The see and the lame walk; . . . the dead are raised" (Matthew 11:4–5). In other words, "John . . . I am the promised one. I do care about you." The words of Jesus were what John needed in his desperation—and they are what we need as well. Because of Jesus, I never need wonder . . . Does God care? (1 Peter 5:7).

At times in life, each of us faces painful situations. Circumstances beyond our control—war, an automobile accident, excruciating illness, prejudice, poverty, rebellious children, an unhappy spouse, or a sudden untimely death.

It's important to remember . . . that God is the perfect Steward. He is in charge of all of life and is fully reliable even while we doubt. He has promised to give strength for each trial. He will not allow us to suffer . . . or even live . . . one day beyond our time. However, we must not die . . . before we die.

Robert Browning said it eloquently:

There is but one way . . . to browbeat this world,
Dumb-founder doubt . . . and repay scorn in *kind*—
To go on *trusting* . . . 'til faith moves mountains.

So . . . don't doubt in the dark . . . *what God has revealed in the light.*

2

Pick Up
the Pieces

My high school buddy was special. Whatever I could do, he could do . . . better. I swam twenty laps at the local YMCA, and he would swim forty laps. I would earn a B+ in history, and my friend Schyler would pull an A+. Both of us also sensed the call to serve in some form of ministry.

Because my father had been influenced by D. L. Moody, he urged me to go to his Chicago school, whereas Schyler enrolled at Wheaton College. Though separated by a hectic college schedule and some forty miles, we still kept in touch. After graduation and further education, we both became pastors.

Both of us were afflicted with life-threatening physical problems. I fought a bout with testicular cancer involving two surgeries and a series of thirty radiation treatments. My situation was so bad that I was told I might not live the year out, and if I did, I could not father children.

Schyler developed a brain tumor. Contrary to the doctor's predictions, I recovered from my illness, but Schyler did not. He died before he was forty years of age.

Early in life, I wrestled with the question of pain. I struggled with "Why do bad things happen to good people?" I confess that I still struggle daily with questions concerning human suffering.

Life is like a giant tapestry. From the upper side, the picture and message is clear and at times even beautiful. However, from the underside, it's a maze of tangled, confusing threads. Mysteries abound.

William Cowper wrote about life's mysteries:

> *God moves in a mysterious way*
> *His wonders to perform;*
> *He plants His footsteps in the sea,*
> *And rides upon the storm.*

> *Judge not the Lord by feeble sense,*
> *But trust Him from His grace;*
> *Behind a frowning providence*
> *He hides a smiling face.*

> *His purposes will ripen fast,*
> *Unfolding every hour:*

The bud may have a bitter taste,
But sweet will be the flower.

Blind unbelief is sure to err,
And scan His works in vain:
God is His own interpreter,
And He will make it plain.

In this life "we see through a glass, darkly" (1 Corinthians 13:12 KJV). While John languished in prison, King Herod and Herodias lived it up. At a birthday bash for Herod, Salome, the daughter of Herodias, danced. According to Matthew 14, Herod was mesmerized by her moves and glibly promised anything she wanted. Prompted by her mother, who was out to get John, Salome asked, "Give me John the Baptist's head here on a platter" (Matthew 14:8).

Feeling trapped, Herod had John beheaded to satisfy Salome's request. Matthew 14:12 reads, "Then his disciples came and took away the body and buried it, and went and told Jesus."

There are those times in each of our lives . . . when by sheer faith, we must in our confusion and helplessness . . . pick up the pieces . . . and go . . . and tell Jesus.

3

Caravaggio's
Doubting Thomas

I have a copy of Caravaggio's masterpiece, *Doubting Thomas*. The artist's real name was Michelangelo Merisi, from a farming community east of Milan named Caravaggio. He lived part of his life during the lifetime of Michelangelo Buonarroti of Florence (1475–1564), and therefore, knew a lot about that renowned painter, sculptor, architect, and poet.

Caravaggio's painting pictures Jesus after the Resurrection with three of His disciples. It's clear which one is Thomas, because the focus is on him literally poking his fingers into the open, wounded side of Jesus.

The Scripture records the words of Jesus to Thomas, "Reach your finger here, and look at My hands; and reach your hand here, and put it into My side. *Do not* be unbelieving, but believing" (John 20:27, emphasis added). In other words, "Thomas, believe and don't doubt."

Doubting is a reasonable response to many situations in life. Doubting can even at times save us from acting hastily or from making a commitment to an unworthy cause. Doubt in this context is *not* an enemy of faith.

Scripture implies that doubt began in the heart of Lucifer when he doubted God's authority and aspired to "be like the Most High" (Isaiah 14:14).

Doubt on earth was conceived in the Garden of Eden when Satan, through the serpent, cast doubt on the character of God (Genesis 3:1–5). Sadly, Adam and Eve bought into doubt and disobeyed God's clear agreement, which resulted in rebellion.

Even in the Gospels, doubt suggests a *lack of confidence in God.* Peter doubted the ability of Jesus to keep him from drowning (Matthew 14:31). Peter was accused of having "little faith." He doubted that he could walk on water. We are also told that if we have faith and do not doubt, we can move mountains (Matthew 21:21). Faith again is presented as the opposite of doubt.

The doubts of Thomas were ultimately for our good because he established the fact that the Jesus of history and the Jesus of faith . . . are one and the same.

Thomas had listened to the witness of the disciples and to the witness of the angels, but he needed visible, flesh-and-blood confirmation. Thomas verified the fact that the Jesus of the Gospels . . . was also the same Jesus who triumphed over death and the grave. After Thomas fully believed, Jesus said, "Thomas, because you have seen Me, you have believed. Blessed are those who have not seen and yet have believed" (John 20:29).

Both believers and unbelievers experience doubt, according to the Bible. For believers, it's primarily a wavering of faith in the promises of God. For unbelievers it suggests an open, defiant unbelief. The secular world says, "Seeing is believing," but the Bible promises, "Believing is seeing."

4

A Supernatural Attitude

There is little difference in people, but *that* little difference makes a big difference. That little difference is . . . *attitude,*" said Clement Stone.

The story is told of a duck hunter and his sensational dog. Whenever he shot a flying duck, his dog would run . . . *on top of the water* and retrieve the duck. However, his hunting buddies never appeared to notice or comment about this talented dog.

On one occasion, after downing several ducks, he could no longer stand their silence and asked directly, "Didn't you notice anything unusual about my hunting dog?" To which they responded, "Yes—he can't swim!"

Contrary to the view of some . . . it's natural to be negative. Paul the apostle confirms this in his letter to the Christians in Rome: "And *even we Christians,* although we have the Holy Spirit within us as a foretaste of future glory, *also groan* to be released from pain and suffering. We, too, wait anxiously for that day when God will give us *our full rights as his children,* including the new bodies he has promised us" (Romans 8:23 NLT, emphasis added).

We "groan" along with all of fallen creation. Pain and suffering exist as a consequence of human failure. Our world was marred by human rebellion and continues to exist at all only because of God's mercy. The real question is, How can I encourage and cultivate an attitude of faith that will transcend my doubts?

While in a Roman jail, the apostle Paul revealed a supernatural attitude. He said, "The things which happened to me have *actually* turned out for the *furtherance* of the gospel" (Philippians 1:12, emphasis added). Paul didn't doubt . . . in the dark.

Conceivably, Paul might have griped about his ordeal and written:

Dear friends,
*   I have discovered that it really doesn't pay to serve God. Notice where I am . . . in jail, and I don't like it one bit. To think I've been faithful all these years, and I end up in prison. I'm disappointed, bitter, and resentful.*
*   Unhappily yours, the apostle Paul.*

By contrast, allow me to paraphrase his words (Philippians 1:12–14):

Dear friends,
*   I want you to know that this is the first time I've had a missions*

tour paid for by the Roman government. But more than that, they chain soldiers to me for twenty-four hours a day, and I share the good news with them. Every eight hours, they change the guards, and I have a new congregation. Some are coming to faith in Caesar's palace. . . . I'm having a ball. . . . Wish you were here. . . . Keep up the support.

Happily yours, the apostle Paul.

But how can I encourage faith . . . in the dark experiences of life?

Paul suggests two ways. "If God is *for us,* who can be against us?" (Romans 8:31, emphasis added). He reminds us that God is not neutral, but rather is enthusiastically *for us* . . . and that's mind stretching. There are times in life when we are not for ourselves, yet God is *for* me, *with* me, *helping* me, and *urging* me on. The knowledge that God is lovingly disposed concerning each of us is an anchor in the storms of life.

The following verse offers a second promise that is even *greater,* assuring me that God also "freely gives us *all things*" (v. 32, emphasis added). Or . . . every conceivable thing I need to survive and *thrive* amid my difficulties.

These two Bible promises encourage a supernatural attitude . . . and attitude really matters.

5

Eve—
A Woman of Faith

The world's first mother was Eve, "the mother of all living" (Genesis 3:20). Eve began life in a garden with pure air, clean water, and perfect peace. Nature was in sync. Eve's marriage was flawless and her union with God unblemished.

Adam was created directly from the earth, whereas Eve was formed from Adam's rib.

When Eve was brought to Adam, he said, "This is now bone of my bones and flesh of my flesh" (Genesis 2:23). This beautifully describes the union of husband and wife as one flesh.

The next mention of Eve in the Bible tells of the Fall. Originally, she was given the name "woman" because she was taken from man. After the Fall, Adam called his wife "Eve," meaning "life." Why did Adam change her name? The name "Eve" was given to announce a special miracle that would come through her.

The fall of Adam and Eve began with doubt. The serpent said, "Has God *indeed* said, 'You shall not eat of every tree of the garden'?" (Genesis 3:1, emphasis added). Added to doubt was the lie, "You will not surely die" (v. 4).

Softened by doubt, Adam and Eve disobeyed God's command and were subjected to horrendous results (Genesis 3:14–16). Yet . . . amid the darkness and alienation of their disobedience, God promised "hope" *through Eve.*

To Satan, God said, "I will put enmity between you and the woman, and between your offspring and hers; *he will crush your head,* and you will strike his heel" (Genesis 3:15 NIV, emphasis added).

Eve, by faith, believed God's promise, so that when Cain was born she exclaimed, "I have gotten a man from the Lord" (Genesis 4:1), probably thinking that this child would be the future Savior who would "crush" Satan.

But the joy of motherhood was tempered by the results of sin. In the future, Eve would be in subjection (Genesis 3:16). Added to this was the announcement of physical death. But infinitely greater than physical death was the alienation from God caused by sin, which resulted in spiritual death.

In later years, Eve again was overwhelmed with doubt when Cain killed Abel, their second son.

However, in spite of Eve's doubt and failure, she found forgiveness and is *remembered* as a symbol of faith. She again bore a son and named him Seth, meaning "to appoint" or "to establish." Eve saw in Seth the one through whom the Light of the World would come (Luke 3:38). Though Eve failed greatly, God promised that through her child . . . she would participate in God's awesome salvation. *Through Seth and his descendants, ultimately Jesus was born.* Through the Cross and Resurrection, sin, death, and darkness were overcome. Amid intense difficulty, Eve believed God . . . and trusted Him for salvation.

Eve was the strategic link in the family line that led to Jesus. Her motherhood is an eternal forget-me-not to God's ability . . . to overcome doubt and darkness.

6

My
First Goals

Yogi Berra, of baseball fame, used to say, "If you don't have a goal, any road will get you there." Goals are necessary in football, soccer, hockey, and all athletic endeavors. Education also measures success by tests and grades. Ultimately, we pass or fail. Graduation is the goal.

I discovered my *lifetime goals* as a teenager. My boyhood church helped me to translate my wishful dreams . . . into specific goals.

Our local church sponsored an annual Bible Conference featuring some of the famous teachers, preachers, and musicians of America. On a Friday night, August 16, 1940, I thoughtfully surrendered myself to be a follower of Jesus.

The speaker was David Otis Fuller of Grand Rapids, Michigan. He was teaching the New Testament book of James and drove home the point that the majority of people were "hearers" of God's Word, but few were "doers" (James 1:22).

As I listened, I resolved with God's help to become a "doer of the Word."

After the service was over and the closing prayer was offered, I sought out my pastor, who helped me review and crystallize my decision. It was an emotional moment because that decision meant I was willing to do anything and go anywhere to make a difference in my world. That night I began to realize my reason for being alive.

My pastor encouraged my decision and followed it up by thoughtful words of encouragement and choice reading material. As we knelt in the front of the church sanctuary, he committed me into the hands of God.

As I left the church alone, I shed tears of joy and determination to be all that God wanted me to be. I boarded the Number 22 bus at the corner of Utter and Lafayette Avenues and rode it for three miles to the bottom of Haledon Avenue. From there I walked approximately two miles to my boyhood home. The walk was "dream-like," as I felt carried along on the wings of angels.

When I arrived home, my mother was waiting. She never went to bed till all of her six children were in for the night. Intuitively, she knew that something sacred and wonderful had happened. We shared together, followed by prayer, as she too asked God to protect me and prepare me to do His will.

My room was a small unpapered, unpainted, unheated area of the attic. Before retiring for sleep, I knelt by my bed and wrote out my first goals. Here they are, exactly as they appeared on the inside cover of my childhood Bible:

1. Resolve to bring glory to God in everything.
2. Cultivate the inner life. (I must admit that at that age, I had little idea of how strategic this goal would turn out to be.)
3. Disciple as many other people as humanly possible.
4. Win as many people to faith as possible.

These goals were written prior to my sixteenth birthday.

Again and again, I have returned to my first goals as a reminder of my promise to God. At times, I've even wandered, but always to return.

Along the way, I also discovered that "desire," though extremely important, isn't enough to reach our goals. Desire must be accompanied by discipline and determination.

I've never gotten over . . . the life-changing power . . . of my first goals.

7

Augustine's Transformation

A mixed-up teenager named Augustine lived in Tageste (modern Souk-Ahras), North Africa, sixty miles from the Mediterranean Sea, in the fourth century.

His writings today rank among of the greatest of history. Though he came from a backward area, Augustine greatly influenced Thomas Aquinas, Luther, Calvin, and many others. He did this . . . by words. His books number ninety-three, plus hundreds of letters and over four hundred sermons. He lived from A.D. 354 to A.D. 430. His mother, Monica, was a Christian from girlhood, whereas his father, Patricius, professed Christianity late in life.

Augustine, though brilliant, was morally weak. While a student in Carthage, North Africa, he began a relationship with a woman named Una and fathered a son named Adeodatus (meaning "given by God").

During his twenties, he followed a system of philosophy known as Manichaeism, a pseudo-Christian sect that allowed him to live the way he pleased.

From A.D. 376 to A.D. 383, Augustine taught in Carthage, then set out for Rome with his son and his mistress, Una. After a year, he was elected the official professor of rhetoric in the imperial city of Milan. It was while there that he became thoroughly dissatisfied with his style of life.

Augustine wanted to live a moral life, but was too weak to succeed. Even when he sent Una back to Africa because he felt living with her was wrong, he was unable to live alone, and soon took another mistress. Augustine was a slave to his lust and doubted he could ever change.

While in Milan, he came under the preaching of Bishop Ambrose . . . although it appeared that the conversion of a friend, Simplician, really made the difference in his life. This friend not only shared his faith, but urged Augustine to read the letters of Paul to the Christians in Rome.

One day while in a garden in Milan, Italy, Augustine tells of hearing a voice saying, "Take and read! Take and read!" Whereupon, he seized a copy of the Bible and read from Romans 13:13–14, which we have today in English, "Let us walk properly, as in the day, not in revelry and drunkenness, not in licentiousness and lewdness, not in strife and envy. But *put on* the Lord Jesus Christ, and *make no* provision for the flesh, to fulfill its lusts" (emphasis added).

Augustine wrote, "The very instant I finished that sentence, light was flooding my heart with assurance and every shadow of doubt evanesced." Augustine had tried repeatedly to live a moral life, but failed. In these verses, he discovered the way out of his darkness. He resolved to "put on the Lord Jesus Christ." In other words, he appropriated the "strength, purity, and holiness of Jesus" as his own. No longer would he live by his own power. From that moment on, he would attempt to live in the power of Jesus.

Second, Augustine determined to use his God-given *will* to "make no provision for the flesh, to fulfill its lusts." He resolved to say no to sexual temptation. Too often, people fall because subconsciously they make plans to fall. These two decisions revolutionized Augustine's life.

Because of his transformation, Augustine is remembered as one of the greatest thinkers of all time.

8

Contrary Winds

I t's possible to live an exemplary life, and yet be in the middle of a storm. Matthew's gospel reads, "Jesus made His disciples get into the boat and go before Him to the other side" (14:22). The disciples did exactly what they were told to do, and yet they encountered a violent storm. No one is exempt from storms.

Joseph of the Old Testament, though good, was hated by his brothers and abused by Potiphar's wife. While living a life above reproach, he was slandered and thrown into a dungeon. And yet his difficulties were part of . . . his preparation for future leadership.

The apostle Paul, as a prisoner, also experienced a violent storm—on his way to Rome (Acts 27). The ship was grounded . . . the stern broke . . . and all jumped overboard and escaped. On that occasion, Paul, the prisoner, instructed and encouraged all the other passengers.

And what about Job? The Lord said of him, "There is none like him in the earth, a blameless and upright man, one who fears God and shuns evil" (Job 1:8). And yet he suffered indescribably. Though Job was ultimately vindicated, he was never told why he suffered.

We know why he suffered . . . because he was the best man God could find. According to the Bible, Job is an illustration of how a person of faith handles suffering and pain. Job refused to doubt in the dark what God had revealed in the light.

Job 42:10 concludes the story. "The Lord restored Job's losses *when* he prayed for his friends" (emphasis added). It was when Job prayed for his accusers . . . that he was released from his trials. Prayer changes the one who prays.

"The Lord gave Job *twice as much* as he had before" (Job 42:10, emphasis added). Job weathered the storm.

However, there are also times when storms are the result of disobedience. Jonah is a classic Old Testament illustration. The Lord said, "Go to Ninevah," but Jonah fled (Jonah 1:2–3).

Jonah refused because he wanted God to judge the people of Ninevah. These people were the Israelites' enemies, and Jonah felt they deserved punishment.

Jonah also knew the nature of God. He knew that if he warned Ninevah of coming judgment, they would repent, and then God would respond in forgiveness. So Jonah rebelled, and "*the Lord sent out a great wind on the sea . . .* so that the ship [Jonah was on] was about to be broken up" (Jonah 1:4, emphasis added).

The storm was the direct result of Jonah's disobedience. Often trouble is allowed and even sent by God to bring us to Himself.

However, the Bible reminds us that God "makes His sun rise on the evil and on the good, and sends rain on the just and on the unjust" (Matthew 5:45). For the most part, storms are the common experience of all God's creation.

However, storms are also opportunities! The "contrary winds" experienced by the disciples resulted in a greater understanding of Jesus. They not only saw Jesus' power over the winds and waves, but they saw Him in a "new" way. They saw Him as *God*. "Those who were in the boat came and worshiped Him, saying, 'Truly You are the Son of God'" (Matthew 14:33).

Are you experiencing a storm? Review your life and make sure your relationships are all that they should be. Storms . . . are special opportunities.

9

The Man with the Ticking Heart

A burning desire . . . that lasts a lifetime . . . is the mark of an achiever.

Shortly after entering college, John Beekman expressed a concern for people who did not own a copy of the Bible. His interest grew into a burning desire to change that situation.

John, however, faced a major hurdle—a bad heart. Many people with such a handicap would have dismissed the thought of missionary work, but not John.

Instead, he sought the advice of Titus Johnson, the school's resident physician. "You definitely have a heart circulatory problem," Dr. Johnson said. "You may not live past forty."

Without hesitation, John asked Dr. Johnson if he could pursue a missionary career.

After reflection, Dr. Johnson, a former missionary, said, "John, if

God wants you on the mission field, He'll get you there. And if I were you, I would much rather spend ten years of dedicated service on the mission field, where there are many who have not yet heard the gospel, than choose to stay at home and perhaps live longer serving among people who have heard it many times already."

"Thanks," John replied. "That's all I needed to hear." In that moment, John's desire was transformed into a fierce commitment to serve as a missionary regardless of his limitations.

Only that kind of resolve can change fleeting desires into a continuous effort that will last a lifetime.

John Beekman's commitment carried him to the Chol Indians in southern Mexico, where the terrain is rugged, with steep gorges split by swift moving rivers.

When John and his wife, Elaine, went there in 1947, fourteen Indian tribes, speaking fifteen dialects, struggled to survive. There were no roads, no telephones, no hospitals, and no doctors—just disease, witchcraft, and drunkenness.

John Beekman's heart condition could have killed his dream. Instead, he worked so hard that in 1955 the Chol New Testament was complete. Finally, John could not ignore the viselike pains in his chest. He and Elaine went to Mexico City to see the famous cardiologist Demetrio Sodi.

Major surgery was required, and a plastic valve was inserted into John's heart enabling him to continue for another twenty years. In 1973, another valve was inserted, and John again committed himself to renewed service.

Friends urged John to slow down. "I don't listen to advice like that," he replied. "As long as I'm here, I want to use whatever strength I have to be of service in God's work." John didn't doubt in the dark what God had revealed in the light.

At age sixty-one, John died. No one had expected him to live that long, but he had. He was supposed to take it easy, but he didn't. Instead, his work led to the transformation of thousands of Chol Indians and to the translation of the Bible into many languages all over the world.

John Beekman refused to allow sickness to kill his dream. He chose to believe God and . . . defy doubt.

1 0

Success Depends on Your Choices

Success in life doesn't depend on the *dreams* we dream . . . but on the *choices* we make!

Joseph of the Old Testament dreamed of future greatness (Genesis 37:7–9). As he shared his dreams with his family, they envied and even hated him. Their antagonism was so great that his brothers kidnapped and sold him to a traveling group of Midianites (v. 28), who in turn sold him as a slave to Potiphar in Egypt (v. 36).

Though Joseph understood that his "dream" promised future greatness, he didn't realize the incredible darkness he would experience before his dreams came true.

While in Egypt, he again enjoyed early success, only to be abused by Potiphar's wife (39:7). Joseph's dreams ultimately came true, in my opinion, because of his *choices*.

Joseph chose to *serve*. As a teenager, he chose to serve God, his father Jacob, and other people in general (39:4). He had a servant's heart. Jesus, the number-one leader of all time, was also the number-one servant of all time (John 13:3–5).

Joseph chose to be *honest.* Regardless of what others would do, he would be a person of integrity. In spite of envy, jealousy, and slander, he would be honest. When he was harassed by the wife of his employer, he said, "How then can I do this great wickedness, and sin against God?" (Genesis 39:9). Joseph could be trusted with your possessions, children, wife, and dreams. Integrity is a primary requisite for lasting success.

Joseph chose to be *pure.* One day, when no one was around, Potiphar's wife "caught him by his garment, saying, 'Lie with me.' But he . . . fled . . . outside" (v. 12). The temptations of the flesh are powerful and they must be met by a deliberate choice to be pure. Joseph grabbed his hat and ran.

Once again, Joseph was slandered, as Potiphar's wife accused him of attempted rape. Her lies were accepted by her husband, and Joseph was falsely accused and jailed.

Joseph's original dreams promised greatness; however, the dark days leading up to the fulfillment of the dreams were not revealed to him. Yet, Joseph did not doubt in the dark . . . what God had revealed in the light. He believed God and held on to His choices.

Ultimately, Joseph succeeded. While in prison, Pharaoh heard of his gift of interpreting dreams. His success in interpreting Pharaoh's dreams led to his release from prison and elevation to second in command in all of Egypt (41:39–43). Joseph was vindicated and greatly honored.

Eventually, Joseph was reunited with his father and brothers, and he indeed "ruled over them." His dreams came true because of his choices. Success in life *depends* on your choices.

1 1

The
Master Artist

A s a boy, I dreamed of being an artist. Friends in grade school and high school remember me as a budding Rembrandt. Even my high school English teacher was so impressed with my artistic talent that she enlisted me to make animal figures that were used as patterns for wooden replicas for her front lawn. And, occasionally, when the art teacher was absent—and I shudder to think about it—I was enlisted as the student art teacher.

After attending the Art Institute of Chicago, I traveled widely as an artist. In that capacity, I would rapidly draw, with pastels, a large, six-foot picture illustrating some important idea. As the picture unfolded, multicolored lights reflected on the finished drawing, resulting in "oohs" and "aahs" from the enraptured audience.

Watching an artist work is fascinating. Skillfully, the artist applies the background color to establish a foundation for the picture. Various shades and tones are introduced to convey depth and balance. Objects are drawn to lead the viewer to the focal point of the composition. The shapes and objects may appear haphazard at first, but they quickly evolve into a thing of beauty. Out of seeming chaos emerges the scene that was in the artist's mind from the beginning.

Our lives are very much like a canvas upon which the Master Artist is at work. Often, He uses bold strokes and dark colors.

At other times, the Master Artist takes His palette knife and scrapes the existing paint down to the bare canvas . . . or lays the paint on thicker than we would like. Yet, when the picture is complete, we stand in awe at the finished product.

The touch of the Master Artist is always right. He's too wise to make a mistake . . . and too loving to be unkind.

In viewing a painting, one of the problems is that we stand too close and, therefore, do not see it in its true perspective. So also in life, *we need the advantage* of time, distance, and experience. Someday, in eternity future, we'll understand the reasons for the peaks and valleys.

The lesson is . . . don't doubt in the dark what God has revealed in the light. The Master Artist can be trusted. He will use the right experiences and circumstances to make our lives . . . His masterpiece (Romans 8:28).

1 2

Worried Sick

General Ulysses S. Grant tells in his memoirs how he was worried sick. He experienced dizziness, blurred vision, and violent headaches. His entire body ached. However, the following morning, a horseman galloped up to him with a note of surrender from Robert E. Lee, general of the Confederate forces. Grant said, "I was instantly cured when I read the contents of the note. Every pain immediately left me, even my headache." General Grant was obviously sick from worry. It is a medical fact that worry hurts the human body.

John Wesley said he would just as soon curse as to worry, because worry is an enemy. It is an enemy to your health, to your family, and to your future.

Mike Gorman, onetime executive director of the National Health Committee, said in his book *Every Other Bed* that half of the patients in our hospitals are there because of mental-related problems . . . they are worried sick.

What is worry? I like John Haggai's definition:

> The word *worry* comes from the Greek word *merimnao* which is a combination of two words: *merizo* meaning "to divide" and *nous* meaning "mind" (including the faculties of perceiving, understanding, feeling, judging, determining).
>
> Worry then, means "to divide the mind." Worry divides the mind between worthwhile interests and damaging thoughts.[1]

Despite the worry epidemic, there is a cure for the interested patient. Let me suggest two thoughts. First, prayer. Luke 18:1 says, "Men always ought to pray and not lose heart." Prayer is God's cure against caving in. Paul the apostle affirms this in Philippians 4:6–7 (NLT):

> Don't worry about anything; instead, pray about everything. Tell God what you need, and thank him for all he has done. If you do this, you will experience God's peace, which is far more wonderful than the human mind can understand.

Joseph Scrivens wrote:

> *O what peace we often forfeit,*
> *O what needless pain we bear,*

All because we do not carry
Everything to God in prayer!

Prayer is our first offense against worry. The second is an attitude of confidence in a caring heavenly Father.

So I tell you, don't worry about everyday life—whether you have enough food, drink, and clothes. Doesn't life consist of more than food and clothing? Look at the birds. They don't need to plant or harvest or put food in barns because your heavenly Father feeds them. And you are far more valuable to him than they are. (Matthew 6:25–26 NLT)

Occasionally, I recite the poem:

> *Said the robin to the sparrow,*
> *I should really like to know*
> *Why these anxious human beings*
> *Rush about and worry so.*
>
> *Said the sparrow to the robin,*
> *I think that it must be,*
> *They have no Heavenly Father*
> *Such as cares for you and me.*

"So don't be anxious about tomorrow. God will take care of your tomorrow too. Live one day at a time" (Matthew 6:34 TLB).

NOTES

1. John Edmund Haggai, *How to Win Over Worry: A Practical Formula for Successful Living,* rev. ed. (Eugene, Oreg.: Harvest Pubns., 1987), 16.

1 3

Jochebed—
The Mother of Moses

Jochebed of the Old Testament triumphed over incredible darkness.

Jochebed, like Eve, became a mother at a time of great sorrow. The king of Egypt, ruler over the land where Jochebed lived, issued an order to the Egyptian midwives that when an Israelite male was born, he should be killed (Exodus 1:16). This was a major persecution of the Jews.

Jochebed was an Israelite woman who believed even in the dark. When her son was born, she hid him for three months (Exodus 2:2). When that was no longer possible, she put him in a basket and placed him in the river among the reeds. Then she sent her daughter, Miriam, to watch and see what would happen to him. Hebrews 11:23 gives us insight into what was in Jochebed's mind as she hid her baby at the river's edge.

First, it was an act of *great faith.* Jochebed was convinced that God could do anything. She didn't doubt. Second, Jochebed was not afraid of the king's command! For three months she did her best to hide the existence of Moses. Her faith gave her enormous confidence (Hebrews 11:23). She fully believed that God could overcome circumstances and that the king's command was nothing in comparison. Consider how the negative circumstances of Jochebed's life were overcome.

First, Moses *lived!* Despite the king's order and his all-out campaign of death, Jochebed was able to keep her son, Moses, alive.

Moses not only lived, but lived *very well.* Even though his life was marked for death by Pharaoh, another Hand protected him, and—what's more—Moses lived in Pharaoh's *own* house! Pharaoh's own daughter found the baby Moses . . . and took him home to care for him as her child (Exodus 2:5–6).

Man may shake his fist in defiance, but he cannot thwart the plan of God. In the end, God can overrule circumstances so that Pharaoh ends up with the very one he set out to kill . . . living *inside* his very household.

Have you ever thought of what it meant to Moses to be raised in Pharaoh's home? For one thing, the best of Egypt was at his disposal. He had the best education that money could buy. He walked among the elite of the land. He had exposure to the finest leadership training that the world could offer.

But not only were circumstances overruled, Jochebed was able to stay with her baby during those crucial early months. Sovereignly, God rewarded her faith by allowing her to nurse her child, and she even received *pay from Pharaoh's daughter* (Exodus 2:9).

Jochebed didn't doubt in the dark . . . what God had revealed in the light!

1 4

This Hospital Bed
. . . Is My Altar

My awakening to the importance of God's love began through a life-threatening illness during my college days. After several examinations and a biopsy, I was told that I had testicular cancer and needed immediate surgery for the removal of a large tumor.

Because of the malignancy, the surgery was followed by radiation treatments. The radiation left me nauseous, unable to retain food, and extremely weak. In the course of five weeks of treatment, my weight dropped from 175 pounds to 127 pounds.

The school physician, Titus Johnson, a former missionary doctor in Africa, was loving, yet frightfully honest. Carefully, he told me that death was a real possibility for me . . . and if not, the prospects of fathering children were slight.

Those were dark days of doubt. Did God really call me to serve? Was I living according to His will? Was I willing to be an invalid . . .

willing to die prematurely . . . or willing to be childless . . . if I lived?

During my illness, a friend sent me a book about the power of God's love. As I read the book, I began to see my personal need to love God wholeheartedly and to allow His love to become my love. The struggle with cancer, the stillness of the hospital room, the booklet about God's love, and the prospects of dying were all blended together by the divine Physician to *awaken me to the supreme importance of God's love.* Through it all, I experienced a new understanding of God and of the awesome possibility of experiencing His love and sharing it with my generation.

My hospital bed became "my altar." In prayer I reminded the Lord that I desired to serve Him. I prayed, "I want Your will more than anything in life. This hospital bed is my altar . . . I would like to be a '*living sacrifice.*' With your help, I yield myself here and now to become an instrument of your love to my generation."

In the years since that crisis, I have experienced relatively good health, a curious mind, plenty of energy, the unexpected thrill of raising four sons to manhood, and a lifetime of ministry around the world.

Sometime before Dr. Johnson's death, he wrote reminding me that I had experienced a miracle. He was right, of course, but an even greater miracle was that I had been awakened to the astounding importance of God's love—a love that is tender as well as tough, fair and yet firm, with the ability to choose right from wrong.

Periodically in life, I have doubted and tried to climb down from the altar. Repeatedly, I have had to take "the flesh hooks" of discipline and determination . . . and adjust my life to "the will of God."

Life, for me, has been a series of new beginnings.

1 5

The Chicago
Fire Catastrophe

Monday, October 9, 1871, Ira D. Sankey, the soloist and song leader for D. L. Moody, spent most of the day alone, floating in a boat off the shore of Lake Michigan. It was one of the few safe places to be during the great Chicago fire. His partner, evangelist D. L. Moody, fled to Des Plaines with his family.

Both men were shocked. Sankey had just left his home and a secure job in Newcastle, Pennsylvania.

Everything Moody had worked for in Chicago . . . was burned to the ground. The fire destroyed all he had built the previous fifteen years. The Chicago fire consumed three and a half square miles, destroying 1,800 buildings. Property damage was estimated at over $200 million. Ninety thousand people were left homeless, and over three hundred were dead. Robbery, looting, and crime added to the horror of that night.

Farwell Hall, the YMCA building for which Moody had raised the money, was also destroyed. More than the YMCA's flagship building in the United States, it was also the hub of D. L. Moody's ministry.

On the night the fire broke out, Moody spoke to a crowd of some two thousand people, as he did every Sunday evening. The Illinois Street Church was the outgrowth of Moody's mission Sunday school and was also burned. With the massive evacuation of Chicago, Moody's workers were widely scattered and the outreach had to be completely reorganized.

As with all tragedies, it is difficult to know why things like the Chicago fire occur. The fire seemed a devastating blow to the work of God in Chicago. Nevertheless, Christians believe that God is providentially involved in all the events of life. And at times using hindsight, we catch glimpses into God's plan.

Even a casual study of D. L. Moody's life reveals that this catastrophe marked a radical new beginning in his life and ministry.

First, there was a *new outreach* to Chicago. Immediately after the fire, Moody began to rebuild. In two and a half months, he built the North Side Tabernacle to accommodate the work of the Illinois Street Church and also several city missions. By day, the tabernacle was a center for the distribution of food and clothing, and, by night, it was an auditorium for people to gather and hear the gospel.

Second, Moody discovered a *new urgency* in his life. Moody said, "I want to tell you of one lesson I learned that night . . . that is, when I preach, I press Christ on the people then and there."

Third, God gave D. L. Moody a *new ministry.* After the initial relief effort, Moody was free to travel to England in 1873. Unexpected and unplanned as it was, this marked the beginning of Moody's worldwide ministry as an evangelist. For over two years, he preached in the major cities of England with such success that when he returned to North America he was world-famous. As one British pastor said, "Moody took the people of Great Britain in one hand and America in the other. He lifted them up to the glory of God."

Moments of catastrophe . . . often mark the beginning of a brand-new day.

1 6

Don't Crowd
Out Love

"Your greatest danger is in letting the *urgent things* crowd out the *important things*," said Charles Hummel in his booklet *The Tyranny of the Urgent.*[1] Attempting to be a love-filled person never seems urgent . . . yet it's eternally important.

When we think of the great love chapter of the Bible, we immediately think of 1 Corinthians 13, but John 13 is equally important. Jesus said, "A new commandment I give to you, that you love one another. . . . By this all will know that you are My disciples, if you have love for one another" (vv. 34–35).

Tradition tells of the farewell address of the aged apostle John to his first-century congregation. Passionately, he urged them to love one another, as he had often done. "We've heard that," they said. "Give us a *new* commandment." John paused thoughtfully and then deliberately quoted the words of the Lord Jesus given in John 13:34:

"A *new* commandment I give to you, that you love one another." John could think of no other commandment equal to that of loving "one another."

God's strategy for the church is to "love one another." This is the recurring theme of the Bible. The apostle Peter placed love for others at the top of his list. "Above all things have fervent love for one another" (1 Peter 4:8).

Paul also called the way of love "a more excellent way" (1 Corinthians 12:31). John Calvin reminds us that "where love is wanting, the beauty of all virtue is mere tinsel, is empty sound, is not worth a straw, nay more, it is offensive and disgusting."

Tertullian, an early church leader, said: "It is our care of the helpless, our practice of loving-kindness that brands us in the eyes of our opponents. 'Look,' they say, 'how they love one another! Look how they are prepared to die for one another.'"[2]

Often I'm asked, "How can I communicate God's love in a self-centered world?"

Jesus modeled "love" for us. We're told to love *as He loved.* The question is, How did He love? He modeled love in at least two ways: by *serving* His disciples and the people around Him (Mark 10:45; John 13:1–17) and by *sacrificing* His life (1 John 4:10).

Before His crucifixion, Jesus, knowing *who* He was and *why* He had come into the world, took a towel "and began to wash the disciples' feet" (John 13:3–5). Jesus communicated His love by humble service and by His sacrificial death. Jesus, the preeminent leader of all history, was also the preeminent servant of all history. He's our model.

The voice of Francis Schaeffer broke upon the Christian world in the 1960s like a fresh, gentle rain. He reminded that decade that the ultimate mark of a believer is a demonstration of God's love.

Francis Schaeffer told us that we will not be recognized as Jesus' disciples by our elaborate programs, extravagant facilities, elegant music, or eloquent speaking. *Our "new mark" is God's love.* Peter, Paul, and John agreed that God's love is the greatest gift in this world.

Scripture reminds us that "divine love" never fails (1 Corinthians 13:8). Health fails. Business fails. Governments fail. Even friends fail. But, *God's love never fails.*

Peter doubted. He denied Jesus three times.

The disciples doubted. "All the disciples forsook Him and fled" (Matthew 26:56).

It's encouraging to remember that though the disciples failed, Jesus did not!

Michelangelo's famous carving, the *Pietà,* is breathtaking. This sculpture is of the crucified Jesus in the arms of His mother. It has been called "marble in rhythm." However, in spite of its magnificence, this masterpiece will eventually disintegrate, and the artist will be forgotten. But . . . *an act of love* . . . in Jesus' name will last and break upon the shores of eternity.

NOTES

1. Charles E. Hummel, *The Tyranny of the Urgent* (Downers Grove, Ill.: InterVarsity, 1967), 4.
2. Tertullian *Apologetics* 39.7

1 7

God Cares
For You

A beautiful picture hung over my parent's bed in my childhood home. It was a picture of a robin feeding her babies nesting in a flowering apple tree. Underneath the picture were the words of Scripture, "Casting all your care upon him; for he careth for you" (1 Peter 5:7 KJV).

By personal experience, my parents knew the peace and security needed to experience a successful life. However, their lives were anything but peaceful.

My father had fought for three and a half years in hand-to-hand trench warfare in Belgium during World War I. When he returned home from the war, the economy was in shambles and work was unavailable.

When my mother was four, her mother died in childbirth, leaving three little children to live-in housekeepers and eventually an uncaring stepmother.

Though there were many Christians in the family line, both my parents were the first followers of Christ in their individual families.

Shortly after marriage, September 1, 1920, in Wishaw, Scotland, my parents decided to leave Scotland and seek their future in America. Along with two children (twins), they set sail for the States, believing wholeheartedly in God's care.

While Jesus was here on earth, He demonstrated His care time and again. He was moved with compassion as He met human suffering. At the grave of his friend Lazarus "he wept" real tears. His life on earth announced once and for all how He felt about pain and suffering.

Matthew 6 speaks of "the birds of the air," how "they neither sow nor reap nor gather into barns; yet your heavenly Father feeds them. Are you not of more value than they?" (v. 26). Matthew then calls our attention to the flowers: "Consider the lilies of the field, how they grow: they neither toil nor spin," and yet God cares for them (v. 28).

I heard of a hiker walking down the road carrying a heavy bundle of clothing. A stranger driving by in an old truck stopped to give him a ride. The traveler climbed into the truck but kept the heavy bundle on his back. The driver suggested that he take off the pack and lay it down. "Oh, no," said that hiker, "it's enough for you to stop and give me a ride."

As foolish as that sounds . . . we do that too. We bring our cares to God, only to forget to lay them down. What cares are you carrying today?

When I get uptight, as I do too often, my wife quietly quotes her favorite verses: "Be careful for nothing; but in every thing by prayer and supplication with thanksgiving let your requests be made known unto God. And the peace of God, which passeth all understanding, shall keep your hearts and minds through Christ Jesus" (Philippians 4:6–7 KJV).

The words of Elizabeth Elliot in her book *A Lamp for My Feet* have helped me often:

> We cannot always or even often control events, but we can control how we respond to them. When things happen which dismay . . . we ought to look to God for His meaning. . . . What God looks for is those who will worship Him.
>
> This is our first responsibility: to glorify God. In the face of life's worst reversals and tragedies, the response of a faithful Christian is praise—not for the wrong itself certainly, but for who God is and for the ultimate assurance that there is a pattern being worked out for those who love Him.

Are you carrying a health care? A financial care? Concern for your children or grandchildren? Remember . . . God really cares for you.

"He cares for you affectionately, and cares about you watchfully" (1 Peter 5:7 AMPLIFIED). So, instead of carrying your burdens, commit them to Him . . . and *leave them there.*

18

Vincent van Gogh
—an Evangelist!

Artist Vincent van Gogh dreamed of being an evangelist. To prepare himself for this work, he studied Latin and Greek, hoping to better understand the original text of Scripture.

Van Gogh's father, Theodorus, served as a pastor in Zundert, the Netherlands, where he guided a small church in the teachings of John Calvin. Along with his mother's brother, a prominent clergyman in Amsterdam, they urged Vincent to pursue the ministry, feeling that he would find himself in the process.

Vincent longed to be authentic and resisted with a passion conforming to the traditional role of a clergyman. Rather, he longed to identify with the oppressed and poor so that he could communicate God's love.

The Belgium Committee of Evangelization launched a new school in Brussels where instruction was free and students paid only a small amount for room and board. Vincent van Gogh applied and was accepted. The program included several months of training followed by a mission appointment based on a satisfactory completion of the course.

Vincent, however, was older than the other students and never felt accepted. He was also accused of resisting the authority of his teacher and, therefore, was not immediately approved for ministry placement.

His father, along with a prominent minister friend, encouraged Vincent to fill a mission opening in a poor mining area in the South of Belgium, near Mons, hoping that success there would cause the committee to relent and appoint him as a salaried evangelist.

Upon arrival in the impoverished area, Vincent threw himself into the work like a doctor caring for sick people. In the process, he was consumed by the plight of the coal workers who were trapped in a cycle of poverty, disease, and death. There was not a hut in the village that Vincent had not visited bringing comfort, food, and prayer. Within weeks of arrival, he so identified with the villagers that for the first time in memory, he found enjoyment in his work.

Several days before Christmas, Vincent located an abandoned stable large enough to seat one hundred people. The miners filled the stable to listen to Vincent tell the Christmas story. He thrilled them as he told about the forgiveness that Jesus came to bring.

He was successful enough for the Committee of Evangelism to, at least temporarily, nominate him for six months and, if at the end of that period, everything was going well, he would be permanently accepted.

Vincent was so consumed by the plight of his people that after a while he gave up his room, his bed, his clothing, and even his salary to help them. He began to exist on a starvation diet. Even the miners realized that he would kill himself if he continued living this way. At times, he appeared delirious with fever and suffered from lack of sleep. The hopelessness of the people became his hopelessness. When his wages arrived, he immediately spent the fifty francs for food and medicine for the people of the village; when his money was gone, the people were forced to eat berries, leaves, and grass.

Unexpectedly, two clergymen from the Committee on Evangelism arrived from Amsterdam to review Vincent's work. They were shocked by what they saw of Vincent himself and of the way he conducted the work. They rebuked him publicly, concluding that he was insane. They accused him of disgracing the mission and the work. Vincent was speechless. Once again, at age twenty-six, he failed and life held little future for him.

After months of deep despair, a glimmer of hope began to shine through his reading of literature and through sketching the coal miners in their daily toil. This stretched out for nearly a year. Ever so slowly another passion began to grip him as he studied the artists of his day and sketched the poverty around him. Time after time, his beloved younger brother Theo literally rescued him from debt and starvation.

In 1889, Vincent began to paint as a driven man, finishing two hundred paintings in about two years. However, again, few of his paintings sold, and debt and discouragement smothered him. At age thirty-eight, Vincent was drained, indescribably tired, and fearful of being a further burden to his brother Theo and his family. With a borrowed gun, he shot and killed himself.

Did Vincent van Gogh . . . doubt in the dark? Did he abandon faith? Only God knows. His life is the story of a gifted, broken man whose unsellable paintings . . . now sell for millions.

Truly, we cannot measure success by worldly standards or by the results we see in our lifetime. As we look for ways to serve, let's not overlook what we can accomplish for the kingdom as we offer others our encouragement.

1 9

No One
Drifts to Heaven

Many years ago the captain of a whaling vessel in the North Atlantic saw through his binoculars the hulk of a strange-looking ship. It was old and rundown and surrounded by icebergs.

Coming closer to this strange craft, the captain cried out, "Ship Ahoy! Ship Ahoy!" But there was no reply. Going aboard the vessel, he found the entire crew frozen solid. The captain was fully dressed and sat before a desk with the logbook open before him. The last entry revealed that the ship had been in those northern waters for several years—far removed from the usual flow of ocean traffic. It was a floating sepulcher, tossed by wind and waves, drifting from no port to no port.

Life can be like that ship—drifting, without chart or captain. A section in volume 5 of the ten-volume *Study of History* by Arnold Toynbee is entitled "A Sense of Drift." In it, Toynbee described this condition as carelessness about the loss of spiritual and moral growth. He explained that many people who know better deliberately rebel and worship the creature rather than the Creator.[1]

Plato gave another example of this condition when he pictured the entire world drifting like a ship without a rudder.

The person who drifts is usually the last one to realize it. Because we're rational creatures, we begin making excuses for our behavior. We rationalize our actions to the point that we are numb to our own condition.

A study of juvenile delinquents indicates that we begin drifting at an early age. Because of this fact, a life of crime can usually be predicted by the time a child is twelve. And yet most teenagers are shocked and even offended when their elders point out what their conduct will lead to. They simply don't see the direction in which they are drifting.

Another characteristic of the drifting person is that he drifts from a higher to a lower position. No one drifts to heaven. We drift from God. We drift from faith to reason. We drift from reason to senses— and then we drift from the senses to animalism.

Ultimately, drifting results in insensitivity. We become anesthetized to our real condition . . . immune to the touch of truth and deaf to the voice of God. A poet has written:

He was going to be all that a mortal should be—Tomorrow.
No one would be better than he—Tomorrow.
Each morning he stacked up the letters he'd write—Tomorrow.

It was too bad indeed he was too busy to see Bill,
But he promised to do it—Tomorrow.
The greatest of workers this man would have been—Tomorrow.
The world would have known him had he ever seen—Tomorrow.
But the fact is he died and faded from view,
And all that was left when living was through,
Was a mountain of things he intended to do—Tomorrow.

Drifting can be stopped only by an outside force. Paul was drifting into a life of violence as he harassed the early Christians. But one day, while traveling to the city of Damascus, he was stopped abruptly by Jesus and filled with supernatural power that enabled him to reverse the direction of his life.

The time to stop drifting is . . . now.

NOTE

1. Arnold Toynbee, *The Disintegrations of Civilizations, Part One,* vol. 5 of *A Study of History* (New York: Oxford Univ. Press, 1961, 1964), 412–31.

2 0

Try the Uplook

Phillips Brooks, a famous New England minister in the late 1800s, was known for his calmness and poise. His intimate friends, however, knew that he, too, suffered moments of emptiness and doubt. One day a friend saw him pacing the floor like a caged lion. "What's the trouble, Dr. Brooks?" the friend asked.

"The trouble is," Brooks replied, "I'm in a hurry, but God isn't."

Have you ever felt that way? You are not alone. Impatience is a trait of human nature. Even Jesus was tempted to act impatiently but did not give in to the lure.

When Jesus was on the mountain of temptation, Satan urged a shortcut to obtaining "all the kingdoms of the world and their glory. . . . 'If You will fall down and worship me'" (Matthew 4:8–9). Appealing to impatience, Satan said, in effect, "Forget Gethsemane, forget the Cross, and I will give you the kingdoms of the world *now*" (in a hurry).

Impatience is an outworking of our inner selfishness. Our earthly egos clamor for immediate attention from those around us. Whether we are waiting for an elevator, service in a restaurant, or for the traffic light to change, our selfish nature calls for instant gratification.

Patience, on the other hand, is a divine quality. To the persecuted Christians of the first century, faith and patience were not only desirable, but indispensable. Because the *outlook* was dark, James urged them to try the *uplook*.

"*Be patient . . . until the Lord's coming*" (James 5:7 NIV, italics added).

Some of the early Christians were so eager for the Lord's coming that they became impatient. They had begun to crack under the pressures of persecution. They were beginning to doubt whether their suffering was worthwhile.

The word used for "patient" in James 5:7 could perhaps be translated "steadfast" or "endurance." It suggests not simply the idea of resignation to one's fate, but also the quality of self-restraint. It indicates the need to refrain from striking back.

Be patient, James was telling them, without seeking revenge. No matter how dark it is, stand firm, take heart, and be patient, for the Lord will come.

Be patient . . . because God is at work. James writes, "See how the farmer waits for the land to yield its valuable crop and how patient he is for the autumn and spring rains" (5:7 NIV).

In the spring, the farmer plows, harrows, plants, cultivates, and waits for the harvest. Day after day, week after week, and month after month, he toils over his plants, waiting expectantly for the harvest that is to come. He cannot control or command nature. He must patiently wait for the earth to bring forth its abundance.

To Christians, God is the master gardener and we are His garden (1 Corinthians 3:9). He plants, then patiently waits to gather a harvest from our lives. He suggests that we also are to be patient in life, even as He is patient with us.

Johnson Oatman has written, "So amid the conflict, whether great or small, do not be discouraged—God is over all."

Be patient . . . because "the Judge is . . . at the door" (James 5:9 NIV, italics added).

James climaxes his thought by urging faithfulness in light of the Judgment Day. "Don't grumble against each other," he reminds us, "or you will be judged" (James 5:9 NIV).

James contrasts earthly judges, who are limited and partial, with the ultimate Judge, who is all-knowing. He suggests that it's a mistake to grumble in light of a future day of reckoning. The same blessed hope that enables us to be patient with the world can help us to get along with fellow Christians.

So . . . why should we *believe* rather than doubt? Why should we try the uplook? James offers three solid reasons: Jesus is coming, God is at work, and "the Judge" is at the door.

2 1

Bathsheba—
The Power to Change

You know the sad story of Bathsheba and David. It all began with a look. David lusted after Bathsheba; committed adultery with her; had her husband, Uriah, killed; and then married her. The record is one of the darkest chapters in the Bible, but the story of Bathsheba is also . . . a story of *God's power to transform lives.*

David and Bathsheba had an illegitimate child, who died shortly after birth. After the death of the child, according to 2 Samuel 12:24, Bathsheba bore David another child, whom they named Solomon. The Scripture adds these interesting words, "And the Lord loved him." Why does the Bible make a point to say that God loved Solomon? I believe it is God's way of letting us know that He had forgiven David and Bathsheba. Their sin was confessed, repented of . . . and dealt with. This new child born of their union was to experience blessing in a surprising way.

And God did bless Solomon. Of all David's sons, it was Solomon who was chosen to sit on the throne of Israel after him. Solomon was blessed with wisdom and was used to write three books of Scripture. One of those was the book of Proverbs, most of which was penned by Solomon. Do you remember the last chapter of Proverbs? Proverbs 31 begins, "The words of King Lemuel, the utterance which *his mother taught him*" (emphasis added). Many Bible students believe that Lemuel was the pet name Bathsheba had for Solomon. The chapter is a collection of advice given to him from his mother. She advises him in matters of *morality,* judgment, and the proper behavior for a king.

Where did Bathsheba get such wisdom? How did one who failed so outrageously have the ability and authority to advise the king in matters of morality? I believe it is that God totally transformed her life. Bathsheba was not the same weak-willed woman who had committed adultery with David. Bathsheba was transformed into a woman of character and faith.

Remember especially the final twenty-two verses of Proverbs 31. Beginning with verse 10, we have the description of *the virtuous woman.* Do you think Solomon could have taken his mother's advice seriously . . . if she herself did not exemplify those virtues? I believe that the description in Proverbs 31 is a description of Bathsheba, and it is a miraculous demonstration of God's unlimited power to change a life.

The relationship that began sinfully ended in blessing. God was able to take human failure and work it to His glory. Because David and Bathsheba fully repented, He was able to transform two lives for His purpose.

Bathsheba also showed faith in coming to God for forgiveness. She had to come by faith. By faith was the only way that she could come to God. She couldn't offer to do anything to atone for her sin, for it is "not by works of righteousness which we have done, but according to His mercy He saved us" (Titus 3:5).

And God honored Bathsheba's faith. In fact, she is one of the three women listed in Matthew's genealogy of Jesus (Matthew 1:6). Through David and Bathsheba came the line that was to bring the Messiah, God's Anointed Deliverer.

Bathsheba's life is an astounding reminder . . . of God's power to change.

2 2

Be a Builder

My father was "a builder" by trade. For over three generations, the Sweetings were stonemasons in northern Scotland. My father loved his vocation and gave it everything he had.

After immigrating to the United States in 1922, he became the foreman of a sizable construction company in northern New Jersey. Because he had a "gung-ho" attitude and because he pushed his men for quality and speed, his work crew would jestingly say, "Scottie, didn't you know that Rome wasn't built in a day!" To which he would reply . . . with a twinkle in his eye, "I know, *but I wasn't foreman on that job.*"

Each of us . . . is a builder. To the early Christians, Paul wrote, "You are God's building" (1 Corinthians 3:9). Of himself, Paul said, "I have laid the foundation"; and then he added, "Let each one take heed how he builds" (v. 10). Infinite care should be given to "how we build" in life.

Samson of the Old Testament never built anything that I'm aware of. Essentially, he was a destroyer. Once he slew several hundred people with the jawbone of a donkey (Judges 15:15). On another occasion, he tied firebrands to the tails of foxes and released them among the dry wheat shocks of the Philistines, creating destruction (vv. 4–5). At Gaza, he single-handedly carried away the gates of the city (16:3), and later he died . . . wrecking a building (vv. 29–30). There's no record *that Samson built a thing.*

He was born between the towns of Zorah and Eshtaol, and that's *where he was buried* (16:31). Samson, though handsome, strong, and multitalented, abused his life, destroying himself and others.

Periodically, it's strategic to ask, "Am I a builder?" Somewhere I read this poem, which says it well:

> *I watched them tearing a building down,*
> *A gang of men in a busy town,*
> *With a yo-heave-ho and a lusty yell,*
> *They swung a beam and the side wall fell.*
> *I asked the foreman: "Are these men skilled,*
> *The kind you would hire if you wanted to build?"*
> *He laughed and said, "Why, no indeed,*
> *Just common labor is all I need.*
> *They can easily wreck in a day or two*
> *What builders have taken years to do."*
> *I asked myself, as I went my way,*

"Which of these roles have I tried to play?
Am I a builder, who works with care,
Measuring life by the rule and square,
Shaping my deeds by the well-made plan,
Patiently doing the best I can?
Or am I a wrecker who walks the town,
Content with the chore of tearing down?"

Resolve . . . to be a builder!

2 3

Word Power

Edward Everett Hale, in his story *The Man Without a Country*, tells of a fine young naval officer, Philip Nolan, who with some others was on trial for being false to the service. The court session dragged on. At the close of the trial, Philip was asked if he wished to say anything to show that he had always been faithful to the United States. In a fit of frenzy, he cursed the United States and said, "I wish I may never hear of the United States again!"

The judge and the jury were shocked. In fifteen minutes they issued the verdict: "The Court decides, subject to the approval of the President, that you shall never hear the name of the United States again!" Philip laughed! But nobody else did.

The plan was adopted. Philip Nolan, from September 23, 1807, until the day he died, May 11, 1863, never heard the name of the United States again. He was placed on a ship with orders that he was to hear nothing of his country, nor see any information regarding it. He was transferred from ship to ship so that he never saw the United States again. All because of fifteen careless words . . . uttered in a moment of anger.

Words can kiss or kill. They can caress or cut. They can be a beautiful angel or an ugly demon. Our words can be our greatest asset or our greatest liability.

Bernard of Clairvaux spoke, and thousands of people left all their earthly goods to follow him for the Second Crusade.

Patrick Henry's immortal words, "Give me liberty, or give me death!" inspired a nation to fight for liberty. Words are powerful. "Death and life are in the power of the tongue" (Proverbs 18:21).

Because of careless words, brothers and sisters have fought or grown apart. Children have left home and cut off meaningful communications, husbands and wives have separated, and the best of friends have become enemies.

A young man was suffering from cancer of the tongue. Before the operation, the doctor told him that he would never speak again. The young man paused and then said, "Thank God for Jesus." What significant last words.

May we pray with Frances Havergal, "Take my lips and let them be filled with messages for Thee." Or with David, "Let the words of my mouth and the meditation of my heart be acceptable in Your sight, O Lord, my strength and my redeemer" (Psalm 19:14).

Zacharias, the father of John the Baptist, became mute because he doubted that he and his wife, Elizabeth, could have a child in their old age. Yet, when their child was born and *named John* . . . his tongue was freed and he used his words to rejoice and honor God.

We've all been guilty, not of fifteen idle words . . . but of multiplied *millions* of idle words. Peter reminds us, "Whoever would love life and see good days must keep his tongue from evil and his lips from deceitful speech" (1 Peter 3:10 NIV).

2 4

The Puzzle of Life

J ames G. Hunker said, "Life is like an onion. You peel off layer after layer and ultimately arrive at nothing." Though I disagree with his conclusion, I do understand his doubt. So . . . what is life?

An artist might answer the question by saying, "Life is a picture of beauty . . . or pure chaos." The musician could say, "Life is an enchanting melody . . . or maybe a dismal dirge." The poet might say, "Life is a dream . . . or maybe a drag." The comedian, "Life is a joke." The pessimist, "Life is a lie . . . and love is a cheat."

All agree on one thing . . . life is short. Even one hundred years —in the perspective of "everlasting life"—is brief.

Job of the Old Testament described his life this way, "My days are swifter than a weaver's shuttle" (Job 7:6). The shuttle moves so fast, that it appears as a blur. Psalm 103:15–16 reads, "As for man, his days are like grass; as a flower of the field, so he flourishes. . . . For, the wind passes over it, and it is gone." Scripture compares the brevity of life to the wildflowers of the field or to a speeding arrow, a falling leaf, a darting shadow, or even a vapor that appears momentarily and vanishes. When all is said and done, life is so short that "the wood of the cradle rubs up tight against the marble of the tomb."

For some people, life is *power*. They want to be in charge. For others, it's *money*. Aristotle Onassis said, "It is the people with money who are the royalty of our times," and yet he died disillusioned and lonely.

For some, life is a *game of blind man's bluff*. Around and around they go, hoping to find the proverbial jackpot. Others indulge in pleasure and lose themselves in intoxication. But each of us has only one life to live . . . and we need to make sure we choose what is best.

Thousands come to the end of life only to discover they haven't really lived, but merely existed. Robert Burns, the Scottish poet, wrote: "Life, you art a galling load, along a rough and weary road." Life for many is a huge burden. The person without faith has a burden too big to carry, like Atlas . . . with the world on his back.

That's why many doubt in the dark. That's why more people commit suicide each year than die from the five most common communicable diseases. Millions of people are overwhelmed with worry, anxiety, and fear, seeking but never finding faith, hope, or rest. Jesus promised, "Come to Me, all you who labor and are heavy laden, and I will give you rest" (Matthew 11:28).

Some frivolously claim that life begins at age forty. Others mindlessly say that life begins at midnight. The fact is, life begins when one comes to know God. Scripture says, "This is eternal life, that they may know You, the only true God, and Jesus Christ whom You have sent" (John 17:3). For me, this is the only satisfying answer to the puzzle of life.

2 5

Esther—
A Hero Forever

Esther was a Jewish orphan of sterling character and startling beauty among the exiled Jews of Persia. She was raised by a godly relative, Mordecai.

King Ahasuerus had rejected his queen and sought for a successor among the eligible women of the empire.

Esther's beauty and intelligence was of such a nature that "the king loved Esther more than all the other women, and she obtained grace and favor in his sight" (Esther 2:17). For over nine years, she served as queen of Persia, all the while guarding the secret of her Jewish nationality.

Haman, the king's prime minister, despised the exiled Jews who lived among the Persians and schemed to annihilate them from the empire. In particular, he was offended by Mordecai because he would not bow down before him (5:9, 13). Mordecai, like Daniel, could not in good conscious pay homage to a person like Haman.

Secretly, Haman gained the confidence of the king to launch a purge against all the Jews of the empire. He complained that "a certain race," because of their laws, were different and didn't obey the king's law. Therefore, they should be exterminated. The king, possibly intoxicated, approved the plan.

Quickly, Haman sent a decree from the Persian Gulf to the Caspian Sea and from the Mediterranean Sea to India that, on a certain day, there would be a mass extermination of the Jewish people.

When Mordecai heard of Haman's plot, he sought out Queen Esther. His words to her are famous: "Who knows whether you have come to the kingdom for such a time as this" (4:14).

It was a desperate hour for Esther, Mordecai, and the Jewish race. Apparently Mordecai had been cut off from seeing Esther for many years. He may have wondered whether or not the pomp and power of the palace had changed her. Common people often forget their roots.

However, the story of Esther is of a beautiful, modest woman who was willing to forfeit her position in life to save her people.

There was a law that no one could come before the king unless he extended the golden scepter toward that person as a sign of welcome. Esther resolved to approach the king without a royal invitation, which could mean her immediate death. After much heart searching, she determined, "I will go to the king, . . . and if I perish, I perish!" (4:16).

Esther, with great faith, drew aside the curtain and entered the elaborate throne room to approach the king—and "found favor in his sight, and the king held out to Esther the golden scepter" (5:2). The king asked what she wanted.

Wisely, she waited to share her enormous burden. With all her feminine charm and talent, she invited the king and Prime Minister Haman to be her guest at a banquet that she would prepare. Once again, at the banquet, the king asked Esther, "What do you want? Tell me what's troubling you."

But again, she kept her secret and invited them to a second banquet.

The night before the second banquet, the king couldn't sleep. To pass the night away, he asked an assistant to read to him from the history of his reign. Providentially, the assistant read how Mordecai had saved the king from assassination by two of his subordinates but was never rewarded for his loyalty.

At the second banquet, Esther told the king of her Jewish roots. She also told him that Haman, the prime minister, planned to kill Mordecai and exterminate all of her people. King Ahasuerus reversed his decree, rewarded Mordecai, and hanged Haman.

Esther's faith prevailed. Her courage still echoes through the centuries: "If I perish, I perish!" (4:16).

Esther reminds each of us that God has a purpose for our lives and that He has brought us to where we are "for such a time as this" (4:14).

2 6

Created to Fly

A rancher found an eagle's egg and put it into a prairie chicken's nest. The baby eagle hatched with the brood of chicks and grew with them. All his life, the eagle thought he was a prairie chicken and therefore did what prairie chickens do. He scratched in the dirt for seeds and insects to eat. He clucked and never flew more than a few feet off the ground. He thought he was a prairie chicken.

Years passed and the eagle grew old. One day he saw a magnificent bird flying high above in the cloudless sky. "What's that?" he asked. "That's an eagle, the king of the birds . . . but don't think about it. You can't ever be like that!" So, the eagle never thought about it . . . and died . . . thinking he was a prairie chicken. How sad! Created to fly, but conditioned to scratch in the dirt chasing bugs.

It's a sad fact of life that we are too easily satisfied scratching in the dirt when we were created to fly. Eagles are all around us . . . conditioned to live like prairie chickens.

May we shun mediocrity. The dictionary defines mediocrity as "ordinary, neither good nor bad, barely adequate, poor, inferior." Mediocrity is playing five strings on a ten-stringed instrument! It's a person with jet power doing push cart work! It's reaping ten rows of corn, when acres are waiting to be harvested. Mediocrity is a person with eagle talent thrashing about like a prairie chicken. It's crawling on our hands and knees when we were created to stand . . . walk . . . run . . . and even . . . fly.

Whoever you are, or whatever you do, some kind of greatness is within your reach. The apostle Paul urges, "*So run* your race to *win*" (1 Corinthians 9:24 TLB, emphasis added). Average running doesn't win! Jesus said, "Let your light *so shine* before men, that they may see your good works and glorify your Father in heaven" (Matthew 5:16, emphasis added). Ordinary shining doesn't glorify God. Of the early Christians we read, "They . . . so spoke that a great multitude . . . believed" (Acts 14:1). Passionless speaking convinces no one.

Isaiah promised, "Those who wait on the Lord shall renew their strength; they shall mount up with wings like eagles, they shall run and not be weary, they shall walk and not faint" (40:31).

Because we are created in God's image, and because by faith we have become the children of God, and because the Holy Spirit indwells each believer, we can stand, walk, run, and even fly . . . on eagle's wings.

The familiar hymn says it well.

I want to scale the utmost height,

And catch a gleam of glory bright;
For *faith* has caught the joyful sound,
The song of saints on *higher ground.*[1]

We were created to fly.

NOTE

1. Johnson Oatman Jr., (1856–1926), "Higher Ground," emphasis added.

2 7

The Virgin's
Name Was Mary

Have you ever wondered why God chose Mary to be the mother of Jesus? Mary was a unique person, the *only one* among millions of women to be selected as God's instrument for bringing His Son into the world. She was a woman of astonishing faith.

After Mary heard the startling announcement from the angel that she was to be the mother of the Messiah, she responded, "Behold the maidservant of the Lord! Let it be to me according to your word" (Luke 1:38). Mary said in effect, "Lord, I'm your servant. Whatever you want, I want. Let it happen to me, as you said."

Mary could have doubted. She could have said, "I'm unworthy. I can't fill such a lofty position." Or she could have reasoned, "We don't have a suitable home for the Son of God. Count me out."

But she didn't. In fact, Mary was willing even to lose Joseph because she fully believed God. I am sure that Mary experienced doubts. She must have wondered, *What will I tell people since I have no husband? And what will I tell Joseph, the man I'm engaged to and plan to marry? Will Joseph understand?* She must have been overwhelmed by the multitude of questions.

However, Mary was willing to suffer the embarrassment that would result from her pregnancy. Why? Because she believed God and knew that His supernatural hand was at work within her. The Lord rewarded Mary's faith and submission by sending an angel to speak to Joseph.

Luke tells us that Mary pondered, or literally, *treasured* the angel's words and turned them over again and again in her mind. She kept them in her heart (Luke 2:19).

After the angelic announcement, she pondered the message of the angels. "How can this be," she said, "since I do not know a man?" (Luke 1:34). Then the angel gave Mary proof that her child would be without a human father. What was the proof? Luke 1:36–37 states, "Elizabeth your relative has also conceived a son in her old age; and this is now the sixth month for her who was called barren. For with God nothing will be impossible."

What did the angel say to Mary? The angel said that if God could cause Elizabeth to conceive, He could do anything. If Elizabeth and Zacharias could have a baby in their old age, then Mary could have a child without a human father. Nothing is too hard for God.

After meeting with Elizabeth, she pondered all the implications of being selected as God's chosen instrument.

When the shepherds came to visit the Christ Child and the angels sang, she pondered the awesomeness of it all. Mary's pondering displays a sensitive and submissive woman of faith.

Mary believed in Jesus because she pondered much about Him. She watched Him grow and mature into manhood. She knew that He was no ordinary son. She observed Him develop and begin His public ministry, and pondered all that God was doing. Even when the brothers and sisters of Jesus *doubted* . . . Mary believed.

Mary was also there when the crowd called out, "Crucify Him! Crucify Him!" (see Mark 15:13–14). As indescribably difficult as it was, Mary did not . . . doubt in the dark what God had revealed in the light. She watched the soldiers nail Him to the cross, yet she did not intercede for Him because she knew His divine purpose. Mary knew that Jesus was the Son of God, the Redeemer of mankind, the Savior of the world.

We honor Mary for her purity, submission, knowledge of the Scriptures . . . and because she refused to doubt. Mary was a woman of supernatural faith.

2 8

C. H. Spurgeon's
Glory and Grief

Charles Haddon Spurgeon was the prince of preachers at the close of the nineteenth century. Weekly, over twelve thousand people attended *each* service. His sermons appeared in print weekly in their entirety in the London papers. However, along with moments of triumph were times of terror and depression.

For example, on October 19, 1856, crowds gathered in a new meeting place. It was the largest, most commodious building in all of London. At the opening service, the auditorium was filled with twelve thousand people inside and ten thousand more wanting to get in.

Early in the service, someone shouted, "Fire! The galleries are giving away. The place is falling!" Panic followed. Seven were killed and many were injured. Spurgeon grieved over this experience and never fully recovered from it. This disaster only increased the crowds, and soon all London wanted to hear him.

In his lifetime of only fifty-seven years, Spurgeon published over 3,500 sermons, wrote over 135 books, and edited 28 others. His last sermon was preached June 7, 1891. At age fifty-six, he was prematurely old, with snow-white hair, swollen hands, and a deeply lined face.

Richard Ellsworth Day, in his book on Spurgeon's Life, *The Shadow of the Broad Brim*, says that throughout his thirty-eight years of preaching, Spurgeon frequently was in the grip of depression. Listen to his own words: "Before any great achievement, some measure of depression is very usual. Surveying the difficulties before us, our hearts sink within us. . . . This depression comes over me whenever the Lord is preparing a larger ministry for me."

Spurgeon shed further light on the place of suffering: "The Lord frequently appears to save His heaviest blows for those He wants to use. The gardener prunes his best roses with most care. [Discipline] is sent to keep successful saints humble, to make them tender towards others." Spurgeon continues: "If the Christian did not sometimes suffer heaviness he would begin to grow proud, and think too much of himself, and become too great in his own esteem."

Martin Luther agreed, "Affliction is the best book in my library, and let me add the best leaf in the book of affliction is that darkest of all the leaves, the leaf called heaviness, when the spirit sinks within us, and we cannot endure as we could wish."

Charles Haddon Spurgeon knew great glory, but also grief; strength and weakness; success and failure; joy and sorrow. However, Charles Spurgeon did not doubt in the dark what God had revealed in the light. Spurgeon found strength to carry on through prayer and the promises of God . . . and so can we. "For the Lord is good; His mercy is everlasting, and His truth endures to all generations" (Psalm 100:5).

2 9

Love—
Lost and Found

Collapse in life is rarely "a blowout," but more often a slow leak. In one of his speeches, Edmund Burke describes the decline of character in a person:

> The instances are rare of men immediately passing over a clearly marked line from virtue into vice and corruption. There are middle tints and shades between the two extremes. There is something uncertain on the confines of the two empires which they must pass through, and which renders the change easy and even imperceptible.

Those words remind me of Saul of the Old Testament, who began life like a promising sunrise on a cloudless day. However, because of indifference, clouds quickly filled his sky till in disguise, by night, he consulted the witch of Endor for guidance (1 Samuel 28:7–25), followed by his suicide on Mount Gilboa (31:4).

The church in Ephesus had a similar fate (Revelation 2:1–5). Having "left [their] first love" (v. 4), they passed over into a state of indifference. Though hardworking and vocal for truth, they forsook their first love and moved from virtue to vice until . . . they died.

"First love" speaks of the first days of faith. It speaks of that effervescent period of time when we experienced release from our past. It describes that instance when we realized that God had "removed our transgressions from us" (Psalm 103:12). First love was that period in time when we knew and felt the witness of God's Spirit with our spirit.

An important question is, How is first love lost? First love is lost because of sin. "Because lawlessness will abound, the love of many will grow cold" (Matthew 24:12). Sin is the killer and appears in two forms, *open rebellion* and *indifference* to God's will. Sin builds a wall of separation between man and God.

How is first love restored? That's the all-important question. The first step is to "remember." God is found where we left Him. The call of Scripture is, "Remember . . . from where you have fallen" (Revelation 2:5). *Remember* when we enjoyed God's daily presence, *remember* the satisfying moments of prayer, *remember* when the songs of the faith carried us all day long . . . *remember.*

The second step is to "repent." Holy memories should lead to holy deeds. "Repent and *do the first works*" (Revelation 2:5, emphasis added). Repentance includes a change of heart, mind, and attitude. Failure to repent is fatal. Scripture tells of the consequences of indifference: "I will come to you quickly and remove your lampstand from its place—unless you repent" (v. 5). The church in Ephesus, though commendable in many ways, did not repent . . . and was re-moved.

Today, Ephesus is an empty city . . . a tourist attraction. A great light went out! . . . The lampstand was removed!

3 0

D. L. Moody's Rebellious Son

When children forsake the faith, it causes their parents deep pain, especially when the parents are Christian workers. D. L. and Emma Moody had three children: Emma, Will, and Paul. Of the three, it was Will who caused them the greatest distress, especially during his high school and college years.

While Will was a student at Mount Hermon School, he wrote his father, who was away on a preaching mission, and expressed his rebellion against the faith of his parents. He spoke of his "growing dislike of the Bible."

Even when Will left to study at Yale, he showed little interest in spiritual things and instead planned to study medicine. Will caused continual worry to his parents. Though they wanted him to have the advantage of a good education, they feared for him being "in college, without any reliance on Christ."

Naturally, the Moodys grieved concerning their elder son's defiance toward the faith that was the passion of their lives. The evangelist called this "the greatest sorrow I have on earth." He wrote to Will and told him plainly: "Sometimes my heart is so heavy and sad to think that you have such contempt for the One that has done so much for your mother and father. All that we are or have has come from Him."

While the three children were growing up, the Moodys tried to raise them in the knowledge of Christian truth, but also not to overexpose them to ministry-related activities. They wanted to make Christianity as appealing as possible to their children. Moody steered away from dull piety. And, despite his very public life, he tried to give them a "normal" childhood.

At home, Moody was not "all work and no play." His son Paul described him as a "stout, bearded Peter Pan, a boy who never grew up." They remembered his humor and the games he played with them. They recalled the practical jokes he played on them, such as dropping a squealing piglet through the window of a playroom where sister Emma was entertaining some of her friends.

Will's rebellion took place in the environment of a loving, caring home. Though we can only speculate why he rebelled, it's important to notice that it was against his faith and not against his parents, whom he loved.

What did the Moodys do to win their son back during his days of rebellion? For one thing, they earnestly prayed for God's help. In a letter to Will, Moody said, "I have never prayed for you as I do now."

The Moodys also kept the lines of communication open. It's surprising that their son Will felt free to write them about his rejection of the Christian faith. We know that, regardless of how busy D. L. Moody was, he took time to write to each of his children.

Moody was also quick to ask for forgiveness when he had wronged any member of the family. We see this in his correspondence with Will, and we know it was the habit of his life. When Will and Paul were children and did something contrary to their parents' wishes, they knew that their father would come to their room to be reconciled before they went to sleep. Moody's approach is no sure recipe for bringing rebellious children to the Lord. Still, it shows the example of a father's pursuing love. His children knew he loved them. And in this way, they learned something of the love of their heavenly Father.

Will Moody eventually was restored—in April 1889. When his father heard the news, he fired off a letter saying: "I do not think you will ever know, until you have a son of your own, how much good it did me to hear this." Still later, Moody wrote: "I do hope you will lay hold of eternal life with a firm hold. It seems to me it is the only thing worth holding on to in this life. Everything else will pass away."

Moody's son Will was not only restored to Christ, but also eventually worked with his father, directing the Northfield Schools. His father even offered him the opportunity to lead the Chicago school. However, Will declined, but later became one of the early trustees of the Moody Bible Institute. Moody's wayward son . . . was restored!

William James Sweeting . . .
A.D. 1511

W illiam James Sweeting was the name reserved for the firstborn son in our family, according to our Scottish tradition. The name can be traced back for many generations in our family. That was my father's name as well as my older brother's.

The name *Sweeting* is English, even though for generations they lived in Scotland. On my mother's side, we were part of the "Irving Clan," and on my paternal grandmother's side, the "MacDonald Clan." The name *Sweeting* is listed in the unabridged dictionary. It is a noun, defined as "1) a variety of sweet apple, 2) an archaic version of sweetheart."

The Christian faith can be found in our family rather consistently, though there were lean years when the witness was dim.

Recently, my son, Donald William Sweeting, was studying *Foxe's Book of Martyrs,* which is a record of those who heroically stood and even gave their lives for the Christian faith. Classic illustrations are given, such as Polycarp, Bishop of Smyrna (Asia Minor), in A.D. 69–155. Polycarp reportedly knew the apostle John, as well as other disciples of Jesus. He served as a vital link between the apostolic fathers . . . and his day.

Intense persecution broke out in Asia Minor toward the end of his life. Eleven Christians had been put to death from the nearby area of Philadelphia (one hundred miles away). In an insane frenzy, the people called for the burning of Polycarp. The proconsul entreated the aged leader to recant his faith and escape the hostile crowd. To this he replied, "Eighty and six years have I served Him, and He never once wronged me; how then shall I blaspheme my King, Who hath saved me?" After those final words, he was tied to the stake, amid wood and straw, and burned to death. Polycarp did not doubt in the dark.

Amid the records in Foxe's unabridged edition, I found this paragraph: "William James Sweeting (1511) was burned to death in Smithfield, England, for his commitment to the Word of God." He was part of our family history.

I too choose to humbly follow in the steps of all those who did not doubt in the dark . . . what God revealed in the light.

3 2

Turning on the Power

Imagine a brand-new factory filled with the finest in high-tech equipment—everything that's needed to manufacture quality products. Then suppose a visitor enters the factory and comments on the beauty of the machines but wonders why the machines are not running. No one knows, the workers tell him.

"Why not oil the machines?" the man suggests. They do. But still nothing happens.

A little later another visitor comments on the superb layout of the facilities. But the machines aren't running. "I think you need some drapes and a few pictures on the wall," he says. So these are added. The place looks better, but still none of the equipment moves.

Other visitors offer suggestions one by one—stained glass windows, an organ, even a steeple—still nothing works. The machinery remains idle.

Finally, someone asks, "Did anyone turn on the power?" Turn on the power? Of course, that's it! Sure enough, when someone switches on the master controls, the machines begin to operate. Soon the factory begins to produce.

"How simple," you say, and you are right. But just as the factory must have power to produce, so we need God's power to live life successfully.

What a revolutionary difference the Day of Pentecost made in the lives of the first Christians. Those doubting, timid followers were transformed into believing, bold proclaimers.

When D. L. Moody was visiting England, he heard Henry Varley say: "The world has yet to see what God will do with a man who is fully and wholly consecrated to the Holy Spirit."

Moody thought, *He said, "a man." He did not say "a great man," nor "a learned man," nor "a rich man," but simply "a man." I am a man and it lies within the man himself whether he will or will not make that entire and full consecration. I will try my utmost to be that man.*

On another occasion, Moody spoke further about what it means to be filled by God the Holy Spirit.

I believe firmly that the moment our hearts are emptied of pride and selfishness and ambition and everything that is contrary to God's Word, the Holy Spirit will fill every corner of our hearts. But if we are full of pride and conceit and ambition and the world, there is no room for the Spirit of God. We must be emptied before we can be filled.

Moody also recognized a difference between the *indwelling* of the

Holy Spirit at conversion and a *filling with power.* "The child of God who has been cleansed by the blood of Christ is a dwelling place of the Holy Ghost. But yet he may not experience the fullness of power."

"There are two ways to dig a well," D. L. Moody was fond of saying. "One way is to dig until you find water and then work to pump it out. Another is to go to a lower strata of earth, then strike water and watch the water rise on its own. The latter is an artesian well. The Christians we want are those who are like artesian wells."

Why not . . . "turn on the power?" Ask God the Spirit to have full control of your life . . . and you will experience . . . divine power.

3 3

Only That Which
Is Eternal . . . Matters

"Nothing could ever matter again but that which is eternal," wrote Amy Carmichael. That was her response as a teenager as she returned home from a respectable church on a misty Sunday morning in Belfast, Ireland.

While walking home, she met an elderly street woman carrying what seemed like an incredible bundle. Without a second thought, she offered to help the woman, only to recoil at what she thought others might think of her. However, in that moment, Amy Carmichael recalled the words of Scripture: "Gold, silver, precious stones, wood, hay, straw . . . If anyone's work . . . endures" (1 Corinthians 3:12–14). Though everything seemed quite ordinary, Amy knew that, in that experience, the values of her life had completely changed. From that day on, only that which was eternal . . . really mattered to her.

Amid all the challenges of life, Amy Carmichael's life offers an ancient and valid prescription. Like most of us, she struggled to learn what God wanted from her. From that sacred moment in the city of Belfast to the last years of her ministry in India in total confinement, she endeavored to experience God's approval and, in the process, gave to all an incredible example of how to respond to the dark experiences of life.

A physical breakdown as a missionary in Japan led her to seek another challenge in southern India rescuing children sold to the gods as temple prostitutes. In speaking of the health of a fellow Indian nurse, Amy Carmichael said, "God help us, if we are not better than our bodies."

Amy Carmichael served in spite of a hurting body. She maintained that the inner person can rise above the condition of an infirmed body. She even speaks of "divine joy" in the midst of pain. "Joy is not gush, joy is not jolliness, joy is simply perfect acquiescence to God's will, because the soul delights itself in God Himself."

Before Amy Carmichael died, she was totally confined to bed. But, even in this seemingly impossible situation, she did not doubt but rather grew in faith. During her last days, she often quoted a hymn that tells her source of strength in adversity:

> Green pastures are before me,
> Which yet I have not seen;
> Bright skies will soon be o'er me,
> Where darkest clouds have been.

My hope I cannot measure,
My path to life is free;
My Saviour has my treasure,
And *He will walk with me.*[1]

Jesus was Amy's life, her source of daily strength, and her all-consuming passion. This relationship with Christ made the difference in her suffering. Remember, the spirit of a person can rise above the limitations of a hurting body.

NOTE

1. Anna L. Waring (1820–1910), "In Heavenly Love Abiding," italics added.

34

Thank You, Billy

No one in all of human history has spoken to as many people face-to-face as Billy Graham. Though some secular and spiritual leaders have enjoyed large audiences for a decade or two, none has equaled Billy's fifty years of mass appeal.

It was in 1945, while I was a college student, that I first heard Billy at a Saturday night youth rally in Chicago. I left knowing I had heard someone special. Since then, I have attended scores of his crusades over five decades.

I'm thankful to Billy for several reasons. First, from the beginning, he has given full credit to God for his success.

Often I've heard him quote, "I am the Lord: that is my name: and my glory will I not give to another" (Isaiah 42:8 KJV). In every contact I have had with Billy Graham, I've come away refreshed by his modesty.

Second, Billy has remained true to the gospel. Whether on his broadcast *The Hour of Decision*, his many articles and books, or in media interviews, Billy has consistently stated, "The Bible says . . ."

His unswerving faith in the Bible as the Word of God has inspired millions. His focus on Jesus—His death for sinners and His resurrection—has roused the church worldwide to stick to the basics.

Third, Billy Graham has consistently modeled integrity. Aware of past scandals and the skepticism of a secular world, Billy and his teammates formulated guidelines for themselves. A serious start was made in November 1948, while in Modesto, California. William Martin, in his book *A Prophet with Honor*, refers to this statement as the "Modesto Manifesto."

The team seriously worked at maintaining financial integrity. They determined to live on a reasonable salary rather than receive "love offerings" during their crusades. They turned over the management of the finances of their crusades to local organizations. Honesty was the goal, whether reporting attendance, offerings, or results.

Fourth, Billy and his partners resolved morally to guard against even the "appearance of evil." Being handsome and in the spotlight, they promised to avoid, where humanly possible, being alone with someone of the opposite sex other than their spouses.

Though other concerns were part of the Modesto deliberations, a determination was also made to focus on sharing the "good news" rather than defending themselves, debating with critics, or retaliating. Of course, no one in this life is faultless, yet in spite of differences, fair-minded people are compelled to acknowledge their integrity.

Fifth, Billy Graham has been creative. Wisely, he has identified with gifted people from around the world to reach this generation. He has channeled millions to the needs of the world through the Billy Graham Evangelistic Association. He has articulated the gospel through *Decision* magazine, best-selling books, World Wide Pictures, *Christianity Today*, The Billy Graham Center at Wheaton, and the Training Center in Asheville, North Carolina.

Ministries of this magnitude don't just happen. They're the result of Spirit-led vision and businesslike application. Each facet, like spokes of a wheel, contributes to reaching this generation.

Though he has ministered to more than 100 million people and walked with the greats of our times, he has maintained biblical values and, after fifty years, has remained virtually unchanged. Though singularly gifted and mightily used by God, he is disarmingly humble.

Lastly, I am thankful to Billy and Ruth for their lifetime partnership. They've been an extraordinary couple devoted to making a difference.

Words are too weak to express our appreciation; however, "as for me and my house," I want to say, "Thank you, Billy."

You Can Be
a Rope Holder

No one in the village of Paulersbury, England, expected William Carey to become a missionary. Carey confessed that he was a boisterous teenager. But on February 10, 1779, he experienced a spiritual transformation.

Only three years after his conversion, William Carey was speaking regularly at Earls Barton Church, a tiny Dissenter congregation that relied on visiting lay preachers. The apprentice shoemaker had studied the commentaries and books of his employer and with the help of a friend even taught himself Greek.

Carey soon began to question the church's reluctance to take the gospel to foreign lands. He mentioned the subject at a meeting of ministers in 1786 but was reprimanded by the chairman of the meeting, who said, "You are a miserable enthusiast for asking such a question. Certainly nothing can be done before another Pentecost."[1] Carey was crushed by the rebuke, but did not doubt his inner conviction.

Carey remained silent for the rest of that meeting, but six years later he wrote a pamphlet, *An Enquiry into the Obligation of Christians to Use Means for the Conversion of the Heathens*, which refuted the five major arguments against missionary work. Carey reminded the ministers: "It only requires that we should have as much love for the souls of our fellow–creatures . . . as we have for the profits arising from a few otter–skins."[2]

In spite of no promised financial support, William Carey announced his decision in 1793 to give his life to missionary work in India. He challenged the people of his small church, "Yonder is a gold mine. I will descend and dig, but *you must hold the ropes.*"

On June 13, 1793, William Carey and his family went to India with John Thomas, a Baptist and former naval surgeon who had been a ship's doctor for the East India Company. For seven years, they struggled to survive, learn the language, and communicate their faith to the people. His motto was, "Attempt great things for God, and expect great things from God."

The first major breakthrough occurred one morning in November of 1800 when a young Bengali carpenter, Krishna Pal, slipped on the steps to the Ganges River and dislocated his right shoulder. Thomas had opened a clinic, since the villages had no access to doctors or medicines. He quickly set the bones and then took the opportunity to tell the Bengali carpenter how Jesus could heal a man's soul as well as his shoulder. After that, Krishna and a friend, Gokul, visited the mission regularly and embraced the faith.[3]

In spite of huge obstacles, Carey's faith grew even though he did not see the fruit of his labor for almost twenty years. Not till he completed the revision of the second Bengali version of the Bible and the establishment of a publishing company and free mission schools for low caste and orphaned children in Mudnabatti, Serampore, Calcutta, and Cutwa did he experience significant success.

Then, on the evening of March 11, 1812, a fire demolished the mission, all of Carey's manuscripts, and all the Bible versions in the publishing company's warehouse. "In one short evening," Carey said as he walked through the smoking desolation the next day, "the labors of years are consumed. How unsearchable are the ways of God! I had lately brought some things to the utmost perfection of which they seemed capable, and contemplated the missionary establishment with perhaps too much self-congratulation. The Lord has laid me low, that I may look more simply to Him."

The secret of his success with the people of India, he told his nephew: "Eustace, if after my removal any one should think it worth his while to write my life, I will give you a criterion by which you may judge of its correctness. If he give me credit for being a plodder, he will describe me justly. I can plod. I can persevere in any definite pursuit. To this I owe everything."[4]

William Carey was a rope holder. He attempted great things for God. He did not doubt in the dark. You too can be a rope holder.

NOTES

1. F. Deaville Walker, *William Carey: Missionary Pioneer and Statesman* (Chicago: Moody, 1951), 54n. 1.
2. William Carey, *An Enquiry into the Obligations of Christians to Use Means for the Conversion of the Heathens* (1792; reprint, Dallas: Criswell, 1988), 53.

3. Walker, *William Carey*, 181–83.
4. Walker, *William Carey*, 232.

3 6

Joni Earickson Tada

Many owe the significance of their lives to their trials. We're usually at our best when *the way is steep* . . . not when perched on the summit.

Joni Earickson Tada has been a longtime friend. I remember reading about her shortly after her diving accident. Since that day, Joni has been disabled, unable to use her hands and confined to a wheelchair. However, out of her disability has emerged a strong faith and phenomenal usefulness.

Occasionally, I was privileged to host Joni at some of our conferences. Not only is she confined to a wheelchair, but she's unable to comb her hair or button buttons.

Just before sharing with a large congregation she asked, "Dr. S., would you adjust my wrist watch so that I can see the time . . . and know when to finish?" Joni couldn't even turn her wrist to look at her watch.

Yet, in spite of her limitations, she has developed a healthy soul. Her mind is keen and her speaking is strong. She excels in music and art, and paints by holding the brush in her mouth, between her teeth. Amid enormous limitations she excels. She illustrates a life of faith . . . of believing when it hurts.

I heard Joni share concerning prayer several years ago. Her family took her on a field trip picnic. They left Joni in her mechanized wheelchair by a campfire as they explored the area.

Sitting alone, she confessed to feeling sorry for herself and, as she waited, prayed, "Lord, bring your creation to me."

Shortly after praying, her sister returned and sat on a log facing her. As they were singing the familiar hymn, "Trust and obey, for there's no other way to be happy in Jesus, but to trust and obey," a black bear came out of the brush, ambled around Joni's wheelchair, and even nuzzled her knee, which was inches from the lever of her mechanical chair, and then . . . ran off into the woods.

The girls were too frightened to scream, but Joni said she would never again ask the Lord "to bring His creation to her."

Joni, though human, has learned to live with and maximize her trials. Suffering, although a burden, can be a useful burden, like the splint used in orthopedic treatment.

I asked about her bad days, since we all have them. "Yes," she said, "but in my condition, what can I do?" Then she smiled with a mischievous grin and said, "I could run my wheelchair into my husband's shins." And she laughed again.

Joni has experienced firsthand the reality of James 1:3, "Knowing that the testing of your faith produces patience."

A healthy soul is greater than a healthy body . . . and no one needs to lack . . . a healthy soul.

3 7

How to Have
a Happy Day

Let me suggest a recipe for a happy day.

1. Start each day reading a chapter of the Bible. What food is to the body, the Bible is to your spirit. If possible, at a set time, in a reasonably quiet place, read the Bible. D. L. Moody said, "The Bible will keep you from sin, or sin will keep you from the Bible."

2. Cultivate the habit of daily prayer. Prayer is our personal communion with God. It is a two-way conversation—listening as well as talking to Him. When I pray, I try to include adoration, confession, thanksgiving, and supplication. The word ACTS helps me remember these four areas.

3. Resolve to help someone each day. Psalm 37:3 suggests, "Trust in the Lord, and *do* good." The best cure for stress is activity

for the good of others. Worry, not work, kills people. Work is healthy. The apostle Paul, Timothy, and Titus all encourage us to do good works. "Remind them to be subject to rulers and authorities, to obey, to be ready for every good work" (Titus 3:1).

4. Complete some task that you have delayed to do. Delaying what we ought to do deprives us of peace and poise. "Do it now," whenever possible, is a good habit. Throughout history, it has been the inaction of those who could have acted and the silence of those who should have spoken that has allowed evil to have a field day. Do what you know must be done today.

5. Practice the art of complimenting someone each day. Mark Twain said, "I can go for two months on one good compliment." Wherever possible and honest, use "life" words rather than "death" words.

6. Review your blessings. Someone has written, "I had the blues because I had no shoes; till upon the street I met a man who had no feet." Count your blessings today. Look around you. Be grateful for your loved ones, your job, your country, your health, your possessions, your church, the Bible, and your personal faith.

7. Lastly, don't be afraid to be happy. Enjoy your position as a child of God. The apostle Paul reminds us that we are the children of God. "And if children, then heirs—heirs of God and joint heirs with Christ" (Romans 8:17). And besides all this, heaven is our ultimate home . . . and that's worth being happy about!

For the most part, happiness is a by-product rather than the goal. As we do the will of God, we experience happiness. James 5:11 comments, "We count them blessed who endure." Faithfulness brings happiness. If you follow this recipe, I can promise you . . . "a happy day."

3 8

Henry Crowell
of Quaker Oats

More than one hundred years ago, before the Quaker Oats Company existed, a group of millers in Ravenna, Ohio, banded together to change the breakfast menu of America. Until then, the familiar rolled oats we now drench with milk were fed almost exclusively to livestock. Moving those oats from feed silos to our breakfast bowls was a monumental job. The infant industry desperately needed someone with marketing and organizational know-how, and that someone was Henry Crowell.

Henry Crowell came from a well-to-do New England family that, despite its good fortune, was plagued by chronic tuberculosis. At age nine, young Henry stood at his father's grave, lonely and afraid.

After the pastor spoke the words of committal, young Henry

asked to talk with him about life and death. The next day the two knelt in the minister's study as the boy decided to become a serious follower of Christ.

At seventeen, Crowell himself was stricken with tuberculosis, which had killed four family members already. Doctors told young Crowell to quit school and forget his plans to attend college.

For two years, he rested and worked as a part-time shoe salesman in the firm his father founded. During those years, evangelist D. L. Moody spoke at their Cleveland church. Mr. Moody spoke about how God changed his life through the words of evangelist Henry Varley: "The world has yet to see what God can do with, and for, and through, a man who is fully and wholly consecrated to Him."

"Varley didn't say this person had to be educated," Moody testified that night, "or brilliant, or anything else! Just a person!"

Young Crowell thought, *I'll be one of those people!* With his new commitment, Crowell accepted his ruined school plans as confirmation that God didn't need a brilliant servant, just a yielded one.

Still, Crowell's health continued to deteriorate. The next year, in August 1874, he was told to quit his job and do nothing but rest.

Henry Crowell seriously studied his Bible during this time of poor health. He became fascinated by the frequent reference to the number seven. One night he read a passage in the book of Job, "He shall deliver thee in six troubles: yea, in seven there shall no evil touch thee" (Job 5:19 KJV).

He believed that the Lord was speaking to him, telling him that he would not die at an early age. His faith grew as his condition became so critical that the doctor reevaluated his case and made a startling recommendation: "You have to live outdoors for the next seven years!"

Crowell acted on the doctor's recommendation and went west to the Dakotas to regain his health. Often he experienced loneliness, especially when his fiancée's mother, believing he was dying, persuaded her daughter to break their engagement. But it wasn't God's will for him to die. Instead, Crowell slowly regained his health.

By the fourth year, he began to use his business sense to buy and sell farmland in South Dakota. But during the last year of his exile, a dry spell shriveled his wheat crop from twenty-five bushels per acre to eleven.

Is God moving me from farming? Crowell wondered. Within days, a man offered to buy his prize-winning Percheron horses, as well as his land, allowing Crowell to return to Cleveland. "I felt that I was now in good health," he wrote, "but I would wait and see what God would do next. I knew He would show me what He wanted."

And God did. Within thirty days of the sale, a man offered to sell Crowell a Quaker's mill at Ravenna, Ohio. "I doubt if it will make a success," the man admitted. But Crowell thought differently. In his past seven years, he had learned not to doubt . . . but to live by faith.

As early as 1882, Mr. Crowell outlined a plan for his newly acquired mill: "To make better oatmeal than has ever been made, and to combine such companies as are interested and willing into a chartered company."

Crowell's plans were big. "The general company should displace old names with a single trade market. To this end, it must do educational work, and create an oat demand where none exists. It is only by such a broad distribution and central management that we can avoid the perils of panic, competition, or disaster to some one plant or other."

His plan was so innovative that it took him twenty-five years to convince the small mill owners to give up their petty rivalries and organize under the Quaker Oats Company. Those were twenty-five years of patient waiting and gentle determination. Crowell did not doubt what God had revealed to him.

In 1888, the Crowell family moved from Cleveland to Chicago because the general office of the Oats Millers Association was established there.

Ten years later, the Crowell family came under the dynamic teaching of William R. Newell of the Moody Bible Institute. His teaching revolutionized the lives of the Crowell family. At the same time, the Quaker Oats Company was revolutionizing the world's breakfast habits. By 1910, Quaker became a world organization, the first American food processor to reach this pinnacle.

Once his fortune was made, Crowell became a businessman-pastor, who believed that "a man's business is not chiefly his way of making a living but his altar where he serves the King." His stewardship focused on three areas: his time, his money, and his social action. For more than forty years he gave 65 percent of his income and a great deal of his time to Christian work.

Crowell adopted the Moody Bible Institute in 1901, joining its board of trustees. Three years later he was elected its president—a post he held for forty years.

Henry Parsons Crowell's influence on Moody Bible Institute lasted for approximately sixty-five years, first through himself (1901–44) and then through his gifted son, Henry Coleman Crowell, who served as a full-time employee beginning in 1923. In 1925, Coleman Crowell became assistant to the president, and then executive vice-president in 1946.

The vow young Henry Crowell made in 1874 lasted more than seventy years till his death in 1944. At age fifty-five, Mr. Crowell wrote on his desk pad, "If my life can always be lived, so as to please Him, I will be superbly happy."

Henry Crowell worked through his doubts . . . to become a person of extraordinary faith.[1]

NOTE

1. For a history of Crowell, see Richard Ellsworth Day, *A Christian in Big Business: The Life Story of Henry Parsons Crowell* (Chicago: Moody, 1946). The original title of this book is *Breakfast Table Autocrat*.

Humpty-Dumpty
Was Pushed

The graffiti on the old brick city building offered a variety of messages to those passing. Among them, in bold, black letters: "Humpty-Dumpty was pushed."

Blaming others isn't new. When confronted with disobedience in the Garden of Eden, Adam blamed his wife and God in one sentence, "The woman you put here with me—she gave me some fruit from the tree, and I ate it" (Genesis 3:12 NIV).

Eve didn't do any better. She said, "The serpent deceived me, and I ate" (Genesis 3:13 NIV).

After the assassination of President John Kennedy, I was sitting in a barber's chair for a haircut when the barber asked, "Why did God do it?"

I answered, "Don't blame God. A man named Lee Harvey Oswald did it."

Few criminals admit their guilt. Many insist that they were framed and the real culprit got away. "I have spent the best years of my life giving people the lighter pleasures, helping them have a good time, and all I get is abuse, the existence of a haunted man," lamented Al Capone when apprehended.

Excuses usually only satisfy the people who make them. Yet for many, making excuses is a way of life, as common as taking a breath or going to sleep at night. We are a nation of excuse makers.

The dictionary says that to excuse someone is to "regard or judge with indulgence . . . to pardon or forgive" his actions.

There is a difference between a "reason" and an "excuse." Reasons, for the most part, are real and sincere. An excuse is a weak reason, at best, and at worst . . . a lie.

When Adam and Eve passed the blame for their actions, they were making an excuse. Genesis 3:6 gives the reason for the actions. "When the woman saw that the fruit of the tree was good for food and pleasing to the eye, and also desirable for gaining wisdom, she took some and ate it. She also gave some to her husband, who was with her, and he ate it" (NIV).

When Joseph Stalin was asked to do something he didn't want to do, he would say, "I can't . . . I have to tie up my milk."

When asked what he meant by that, he would laugh and say, "When you don't want to do something, one excuse is just as good as another."

Each of us can recall excuses we've made. But excuse making is a fatal habit, guaranteed to be detrimental—to us and to our relationships. Making excuses drains us of self-confidence and fosters doubt and discouragement in those around us.

As a former pastor, I laughed out loud when I read one church's ideas for counteracting excuses in this little essay called "No Excuse Sunday":

> Cots will be placed in the foyer for those who say, "Sunday is my only day to sleep in." We have steel helmets for those who say, "The roof would cave in if I ever came to church."
>
> Blankets will be furnished for those who think the church is too cold, and fans for those who say it is too hot. We will have hearing aids for those who say, "The preacher speaks too softly," and cotton balls for those who say, "He preaches too loudly."
>
> Score cards will be available for those who wish to list the hypocrites present. Some relatives will be in attendance for those who like to go visiting on Sundays.
>
> There will be TV dinners for those who can't go to church and cook dinner also. One section will be devoted to trees and grass for those who like to see God in nature.
>
> Finally, the sanctuary will be decorated with Christmas poinsettias and Easter lilies for those who have never seen the church without them.

The first step to overcoming excuse making is to acknowledge that we need help. Humpty-Dumpty had a great fall. Each of us is a fallen creature. As I accept the responsibility for my failures and accept God's forgiveness for them, I am ready to correct them and move forward.

When we get ready to make our next excuse, we would do well to remember the old spiritual, "Not my brother, not my sister, but it's me, O Lord . . . standing in the need of prayer."

4 0

Jonathan Edwards—
A Master of Prose

The bow of God's wrath is bent, and the arrow made ready on the string and justice bends the arrow at your heart and strains the bow; and it is nothing but the mere pleasure of God, and that of an angry God without any promise or obligation at all, that keeps the arrow one moment from being made drunk with your blood.[1]

Jonathan Edwards was one of the greatest of Puritan preachers. He was famous—or infamous—for his sermon "Sinners in the Hands of an Angry God." In general, history has portrayed him as extreme. However, Jonathan Edwards was infinitely more than a preacher of hell-fire and damnation.

His life included mountain peaks as well as precipitous gorges. He was born October 5, 1703, in East Windsor, Connecticut, to a gifted-pastor father. At age ten, he displayed gifts of logic and expression. During his tenth year, he wrote a tract, "The Nature of the Soul." This was followed by an essay at age twelve on "The Habit of Spiders." As a young man of thirteen, he entered Yale University and graduated at age seventeen at the head of his class, and as valedictorian. His maternal grandfather, Solomon Stoddard, invited him at age twenty-four to become associate pastor of the largest, wealthiest church in all of New England.

Historian Franklin Snyder, formerly of Northwestern University, wrote this about him:

> Jonathan Edwards' claim to distinction is three-fold. He was a master of English prose, able to write in such a vigorous, clear, and moving fashion that by comparison, most other American writers seem dull and inept. He was also one of the greatest preachers who ever spoke in the English tongue. He was one of the few Americans who have made any significant contribution to the philosophical thinking of the modern world. On any one of these three counts, Jonathan Edwards would be entitled to a high place among the writers of American literature.[2]

And yet, at age forty-seven, Jonathan Edwards was dismissed from his church after twenty-three years of pastoring. The *Encyclopedia Britannica* says of him, "He showed at once that he loved books and abstract ideas more than he loved people. He spent 13 hours a day in his study and hardly ever called upon his parishioners except in cases of extreme emergency."[3]

Though Jonathan Edwards experienced deep failure, he bore his humiliation as a gentleman. Turned out of the pastorate at age forty-seven with a large family to support and no immediate employment, he did not doubt in the dark. Rather, he wrote one of his best books, titled *Charity and Its Fruits*, which reveals a loving, gentle, unselfish individual.

Though offered several notable churches, he chose to follow his son-in-law, Rev. Aaron Burr, as President of Princeton University (then the College of New Jersey). His tenure there was brief, as he died after being inoculated for smallpox at age fifty-five, which he probably contracted because of the inoculation.

Jonathan Edwards' prose is of such exquisite quality as to distinguish him as one of the masters of the English language.

NOTES

1. Jonathan Edwards, "Sinners in the Hands of an Angry God."
2. Franklin B. Snyder and Edward D. Snyder, *American Literature* (New York: Macmillan, 1935), 82–83.
3. *Encyclopedia Britannica* 8:19.

My Angel Mother

"Kilmore Cottage" was the name of my mother's childhood home in Carstairs Junction, Scotland.

Her mother, Annie McKerrow Irving, died while giving birth to her third child, leaving her husband, George Irving, to care for my mother, her brother Isaac, and the newborn . . . Annie.

Life was hard in the Irving home and filled with sadness. George Irving, her father, found it impossible to work and handle his three young children as a single parent. At first, he hired a live-in house-keeper who, along with her children, moved in. Eventually, George married a widow with children and brought them into the Irving household. However, living conditions were so stressful that my mother's brother, Isaac, at age fourteen, left home and joined the Navy, while their sister, Annie, ran away, never to be heard from again. The George Irving family occasionally attended the village congregational church. Several of the family are buried in the cemetery there.

Though my mother's childhood had its share of sorrows, she experienced a marvelous conversion in her teenage years. An acquaintance, named Jesse Kay, whom I met decades later, began a girl's club in Carstairs Junction. After several visits, my mother, Mary Rodger Irving, was converted. As a teenager, she was bright, winsome, and committed to spiritual growth. Her new faith made her home situation at least tolerable.

My father, William James Sweeting, after returning from fighting in Belgium in World War I with the Royal British Engineers, picked up his trade as a stonemason. His work brought him to the village of Carstairs Junction, where he worked on the building of a large stone bridge over the town's railroad station. It was there my parents met. My mother quickly shared her faith, telling of her life's transformation. She also urged my father to visit two centers in Glasgow, Scotland—one called Bethany Hall and the other Tent Hall—where he could hear more about the "new life" she had discovered.

Because of my father's war experiences and the chaos of life in general, he was anxious to visit Bethany Hall and was marvelously converted. The change in his life was so evident that his father feared he would be a fanatic. His conversion led to eventual courtship with my mother and then to marriage to Mary Rodger Irving of Carstairs Junction in 1920.

Tired of the wars of Europe and eager for opportunity to better themselves, they emigrated to the United States in 1923.

Though my father was the unquestioned head of the home, my

mother was "the heart of the home." Along with a deep faith, she possessed a loving, cheerful disposition. She gave birth to six children: William James, Anne McKerrow, George, Norman, Mary Beattie, and Martha Jean.

Late in the 1940s, she was afflicted with rheumatoid osteoarthritis. At times, her affliction was so intense that she was bedfast. Her hands became deformed and her joints gnarled, yet even in suffering, she was an overcomer. With the advent of cortisone, she managed with great difficulty to get about the home. Her faith was obvious to all who came to visit. Amid constant pain and discomfort, she displayed a triumphant spirit and a gentle sense of humor.

Her three sons entered the ministry and served an aggregate of over 150 years. In my mother's eyes, serving God and people is the highest calling possible. From time to time, my mother eloquently exhorted her preacher sons, and we would teasingly call her "the best preacher in the Sweeting family." All through her life, till her home-going, she was to us a ministering angel.

4 2

God—God—Yes!

William Culbertson, the fifth president of Chicago's Moody Bible Institute, occasionally said, "My prayer . . . for myself is that I may end my life well."

I first met Dr. Culbertson as his pupil in the fall of 1942. He was the new Dean of Education and I was a green freshman from Haledon, New Jersey.

From his first day as a teacher and administrator, he was appreciated and loved. He was gracious, reserved, precise, yet warm. He loved the Bible passionately, yet conveyed a spirit of dignity and stability. Warren Wiersbe said of him, "The emphasis of his life was practical godliness and he sought to experience for himself . . . what he expounded for others."[1]

William Culbertson was personally invited to be Moody's Dean of Education by President Will Houghton. After ten years of leading the school, Will Houghton's health began to deteriorate. He was plagued by a serious migraine problem that caused intense pain and chronic sleeplessness. The situation worsened until June 4, 1946, when he suffered a serious coronary attack. The following year, June 14, 1947, he died at age fifty-nine.

Dean Culbertson was asked to serve as acting president, while the trustees searched for a successor. Seven months later, February 4, 1948, Dr. Culbertson was chosen as his successor. Modestly, Culbertson responded, "I cannot take Dr. Houghton's place, but I want to be in God's will."

Speaking at a conference in Great Britain, Dr. Culbertson said: "God being my Helper, insofar as I can influence what goes on at Moody Bible Institute, we are not here to train easy-going Christians; we are here to graduate disciples."[2]

Occasionally, I was invited to speak for the Moody Alumni Week during the 1950s and 1960s, and this encouraged a growing friendship. In 1966, I was called to be the Senior Pastor of Moody Church. At the same time, Dr. Culbertson moved from his home in Evanston to Sandburg Village, across the street from the Moody Church, and he became a faithful attender. This led to an invitation to become a trustee of the Moody Bible Institute in April of 1969.

In retrospect, Dr. Culbertson was preparing me to succeed him, but in all honestly, I was unaware of that till sometime in early 1970. Several trustees confided in me that Dr. Culbertson was struggling with lung cancer, though to me he appeared vigorous although bone weary. These trustees asked if I might be willing to be Dr. Culbertson's successor. I was greatly honored, but considered the subject premature and possibly unauthorized.

However, everything changed on November 19, 1970 when Dr. Culbertson invited me to lunch at the Chicago Union League Club. While we were enjoying a tasty meal, Dr. Culbertson said, "It was here at this very table many years ago, that Henry Parsons Crowell and Will Houghton urged me to come to the Institute. I've never regretted coming." That day, Dr. Culbertson, with the approval of the trustees, asked me to be his successor. Several months later, I agreed, with God's help, to accept the position.

The following months quickly revealed that Dr. Culbertson was fighting a losing physical battle, even though his spirit and words were strong. On October 6, he entered the Swedish Covenant Hospital for the third time in less than ten years. The cancer had returned with a vengeance, causing his physical condition to vary from day to day.

On the day of his death, he shared "the good news" with his hospital roommate. He also quoted a favorite verse, "Alleluia! For the Lord God Omnipotent reigns!" (Revelation 19:6). On November 16, 1971, after a reasonably good day, at 11:30 P.M., he quietly said, "God—God—yes!" His prayer was answered . . . he ended . . . well.

NOTES

1. Warren Wiersbe, *William Culbertson: A Man of God* (Chicago: Moody, 1974).
2. Ibid., 59.
3. Ibid., 154.

4 3

Wanted: Intercessors

As I sat musing in my study, reliving some of life's opportunities, I asked the question "What is the greatest need of our world today?"

The answer came quickly: Our primary need is for intercessors. Our need is not primarily for better planning, or more skilled workers, or even more money, but people who believe greatly in prayer.

Church history demonstrates that the decades of growth were also decades of great praying. Yet in spite of this knowledge, our generation suffers from a dearth of prayer. And this situation must cause God to wonder.

An astonishing phrase is found in the book of Isaiah. The verse pictures God wondering why there is a lack of prayer. "He saw that there was no man, and wondered that there was no intercessor" (Isaiah 59:16).

S. W. Gordon wrote about the present ministry of Jesus: "Thirty years of living; thirty years of serving; one tremendous act of dying; nineteen hundred years of praying. What an emphasis on prayer!"

Jesus believes so completely in prayer that right now He is praying for you and me (Hebrews 7:25). In view of the example of Jesus, it comes as no surprise that God should "wonder" that there was no intercessor.

What is prayer? At times, prayer is a groan. Other times it's worship, adoration, communion, and supplication. The simplest definition of prayer is the three-letter word: *cry.*

As a newborn baby spontaneously cries out, so we cry out to the heavenly Father. Paul writes, "Because you are sons, God sent the Spirit of his Son into our hearts, the Spirit who calls out, 'Abba, Father'" (Galatians 4:6 NIV).

Jesus told His disciples that "they should always pray and not give up" (Luke 18:1 NIV). In light of this instruction, it is understandable that God should "wonder" that there was no intercessor.

Jesus taught that we should pray in His name. "And I will do whatever you ask in my name" (John 14:13 NIV). His name represents all that He is.

We are also taught to pray in faith (Mark 11:24). In fact, "without faith it is impossible to please God" (Hebrews 11:6 NIV).

Prayer is the key that opens the door to all of God's resources. We are told, "Ask and it will be given to you; seek and you will find; knock and the door will be opened to you" (Matthew 7:7 NIV).

When we consider the promises of the Bible and in view of the character of God, it is easy to understand why God should "wonder."

Prayer is not easy. Richard Newton wrote:

The principal cause of my leanness and unfruitfulness is owing to an unaccountable backwardness to prayer. I can write or read or converse or hear with a ready heart; but prayer is more spiritual and inward than any of these, and the more spiritual any duty is, the more my carnal heart is apt to start from it.

E. M. Bounds, a Methodist minister in the late 1800s, left his secure pastorate to arouse others to the need for prayer. He understood why Christians neglected prayer. Bounds wrote:

Praying is spiritual work; and human nature does not like taxing, spiritual work. Human nature wants to sail to heaven under a favoring breeze, a full, smooth sea . . . So we come to one of the crying evils of these times, maybe of all times—little or no praying. Of these two evils, perhaps little praying is worse than no praying. Little praying is a kind of make-believe, a salve for the conscience, a farce and a delusion.

Prayer is an awesome privilege and a sacred trust. May we resolve to be intercessors.

44

The Thistle—
Scotland's Emblem

A very long time ago, so the story goes, Scotland was visited by Viking explorers and warriors.

Once, while a band of Scots were resting in a field overnight, a group of Vikings prepared to attack them.

As the Viking warriors approached the place where the Scots were resting, they had to pass through a large patch of prickly thistles, which caused them such pain that their cries aroused the Scots . . . who put them to flight.

From that day to this, the lowly thistle has been the emblem of Scotland.

The thistle is a prickly plant with a spectacular purple crown. At times, they're a nuisance to farmers, and yet dazzling, especially when a goldfinch perches on its foliage.

I have several expensive picture books of Scotland, and though the emblem of the thistle appears in each book, no one felt it important enough to write about the lowly thistle, maybe because some varieties are so unpopular. The thistle was firmly established as Scotland's symbol when the poet Dunbar wrote "The Thistle and the Rose" on the union of the Scottish James IV and the English Princess Margaret. The Order of the Thistle, which invested Scottish knights, was begun by James V in 1540.

Over the years, I have collected teacups, spoons, and saucers that depict the Scottish thistle.

The thistle is a true picture of life's experiences. Thistles and thorns are inescapable, and yet even these uninvited experiences bring a beauty and purpose all their own. I would imagine most of us prefer roses . . . but roses have thorns as well.

Life has its "thistles." We get pierced . . . no one escapes the prickly events of life. "Man is born to trouble as surely as sparks fly upward" (Job 5:7 NIV).

In scanning through the dictionary, I found the word *thistle* defined as "that which is difficult or painful," "a thistly set of problems." However, these thistlelike problems also present beauty . . . like that of a rain-soaked thistle sparkling in the sun . . . after the storm.

There are lessons for us from the lowly thistle. Things that we ignore or even consider a nuisance can be transformed into objects of beauty. Thistles are allowed, not to irritate us or to inflict pain, but to enjoy. Even thistles are a part of God's varied and spectacular garden.

4 5

Consider My
Servant Job

The book of Job should nail a coffin lid over the idea that every time we suffer, it's because God is punishing us or trying to tell us something."[1]

Job was the best man God could find on earth. According to the Bible, "there [was] none like him" (Job 1:8; 2:3). Job was God's illustration to Satan of a good man who served God without ulterior motives. Satan disagreed! He claimed that Job served God because of his abundance. "Touch all that he has, and he will surely curse You to Your face!" (1:11), said Satan. God accepted the challenge and allowed Satan, within limits, to afflict Job.

First, Job lost his wealth. In a short period of time, he went from plenty to poverty (1:14–17).

Second, he lost his children. They all died suddenly in a windstorm (1:18–19).

Third, he lost his health. Boils covered his body from head to toe (2:7), so that even his friends "did not recognize him" (2:12).

Fourth, he lost his wife . . . at least for a time. She said, "Curse God and die!" (2:9).

Fifth, he lost his friends. For seven days they comforted him, but then, because they couldn't understand why he suffered, they falsely accused him.

Job's response to the first test was heroic. "Naked I came from my mother's womb, and naked shall I return there. The Lord gave, and the Lord has taken away; blessed be the name of the Lord" (1:21).

Job's response to the second attack was also remarkable. "'Shall we indeed accept good from God, and shall we not accept adversity?' In all this Job did not sin with his lips" (2:10).

Although sickness and pain are often due to the sin of the sufferer and to the sinful conditions of our fallen world, it is not *always* so. The book of Job is a giant declaration that God's people . . . suffer at times for other reasons.

Job never knew why he suffered. We know because we have the revelation of Scripture. Job's friends concluded that his sickness was the result of hidden or unconfessed sin. However, God rebuked Job's friends and affirmed Job. "The Lord said to Eliphaz the Temanite, 'My wrath is aroused against you and your two friends, for you have not spoken of Me what is right, as My *servant Job has*'" (42:7). Job lost everything . . . except God, because he never denied Him.

The reasons for Job's sufferings are not given directly, but indirectly.

1. As a result of his afflictions, he experienced a new vision of God (v. 5). This was a definite benefit from his sufferings.
2. The vision of God resulted in an attitude of repentance and contrition (v. 6).
3. The book of Job, which chronicles his sufferings, provides instruction regarding the affliction of God's people.
4. His life was enlarged (Psalm 14:7). "And the Lord restored Job's losses when he prayed for his friends. Indeed the Lord gave Job twice as much as he had before" (Job 42:10; see also vv. 11–17). God enlarged Job's life as a result of his faith.

Against indescribable loss and inexpressible pain, Job believed God. What did God want from Job? He wanted his trust. Amid unexplained affliction, Job did not doubt in the dark what God had revealed in the light.

NOTE

1. Philip Yancey, *Where Is God When It Hurts?* (Grand Rapids: Zondervan, 1988).

He Who
Laughs . . . Lasts

A chuckle a day may not keep the doctor away, but it sure does make those times in life's waiting room a little more bearable," said Anne Schaef. We do not stop laughing because we're old, but rather we grow old because we stop laughing! "Laughing is the sensation of feeling good all over and showing it principally in one spot," said Josh Billings.

Of all the creatures God created, only man is capable of laughing. Laughter is therapeutic!

George Vaillant, who studied how a large group of male Harvard College graduates used emotional defenses, consistently found that a sense of humor is associated not only with good physical health, but also with superior psychological adjustment. Vaillant considers humor to be one of the best coping mechanisms available to us. . . . We use humor both to recognize hard realities and protect ourselves from their inherent sorrow and hurt.[1]

I recall a Sunday service in one of my pastorates when the choirmaster introduced our hand bell choir. Inadvertently, he said, "And now . . . the Hand *Ball* Choir." We enjoyed a good laugh.

On another occasion, our church sanctuary was filled with four thousand people waiting for a concert to begin. The program was also to be broadcast. When it was time to begin, the engineer from the sound room pointed to the conductor to begin . . . but the conductor didn't respond. Unaware that the microphones were open, the engineer blurted out for all to hear, like a voice from heaven, "Tell the old goat to get this show on the road." A shocked congregation broke into laughter.

Here's an anonymous poem:

> *Build for yourself a strong box,*
> > *Fashion each part with care;*
> *Fit it with hasp and padlock,*
> > *Put all your troubles there.*

> *Hide therein all your failures,*
> > *And each bitter cup you quaff,*
> *Lock all your heartaches within it,*
> > *Then sit on the lid and laugh!*

Abraham Lincoln said, "Gentlemen, why don't you laugh? With the fearful strain that is upon me night and day, if I did not laugh, I should die. You need this medicine as much as I do."

Executive's Digest states:

Scientists have been studying the effect of laughter on human beings and have found that laughter has a profound and instantaneous effect on virtually every important organ in the human body. Laughter reduces health-sapping tensions and relaxes the tissues as well as exercising the most vital organs. It is said that laughter, even when forced, results in beneficial effects mentally and physically. Next time you feel nervous and jittery, *indulge in a good laugh*.

They tell us that people who laugh . . . live longer. Maybe that's why comedians live so long. "A merry heart does good, like medicine, but a broken spirit dries the bones" (Proverbs 17:22). Laughter is healthy during good times and especially helpful in bad times. Often I've found help in the poem:

> *God holds the key to all the unknown,*
> *And I am glad.*
> *If other hands should hold the key,*
> *I might be sad.*

NOTE

1. Thomas T. Perls and Margery Hutter Silver, *Living to 100: Lessons in Living to Your Maximum Potential at Any Age* (New York: Basic, 1999), 72.

4 7

My Very
Best Friend

I met my life's partner on a toboggan slope . . . resulting in a fifty-year run. I had watched her from a distance at local church functions and liked what I saw. Margaret Hilda Schnell was shy, pretty, friendly, and spiritual. Our first dates consisted of church activities, services in hospitals, jails, and rescue missions. Both of us were caught up in the excitement of an areawide series of meetings at the First Baptist Church of Paterson, New Jersey. The meetings lasted for forty-one days and we never missed a service. George T. Stevens was the evangelist and was greatly used to bring a spiritual awakening to our area.

It was during that series that we both seriously began to share our faith with others and consider the possibility of future Christian service. Those meetings also gave us a needed excuse to see each other and the chance for an occasional soda at the Paradise Restaurant. Because money was scarce in the Sweeting family, Hilda often bailed me out.

Our only means of travel was public transportation, which meant that I traveled from the town of Haledon and she from the town of Fairlawn. Hilda's parents had immigrated from Seigen, Germany, in 1923, and my parents had come from Glasgow, Scotland, the same year. Our fathers had fought against each other in Belgium in World War I. Both fathers, after conversion . . . decided to leave Europe for America.

As teenagers, I worked delivering milk while Hilda worked in her father's bakery at 14-12 River Road. Often, I would leave a quart of chocolate milk at her back door and find, in exchange, a bag of the best-tasting goodies ever made. I got the best of the deal.

Earnestly, we prayed about our friendship. Under the heading of ambitions, my high school yearbook reads, "To be an evangelist and artist." Because we sensed God's call, we enrolled and graduated from Chicago's Moody Bible Institute. Our time at Moody was incredible. We were challenged to be "our best" and to give "our best." Weekends found us serving in rallies and churches throughout the Midwest.

In those days, I would illustrate my messages by drawing a large, dramatic scene on a six-foot-wide canvas board. Background music helped the audience focus on the scene as multicolored lights produced dazzling effects. The finished drawing became an illustration for the sermon that followed. Both of us enjoyed the work and realized how we were being prepared to serve together.

June 14, 1947, the wedding bells announced our marriage to

each other. Over the years, our love has grown increasingly. In looking back over the years, I could not have found a more fitting partner. Her steadfast love for me and our children has been a source of enormous stability and strength.

We view our partnership as a special gift from God. We do not pretend even for a moment that we were bright enough to make the right choices. However, with great gratitude—and utter humility—we give thanks.

4 8

Moody's Last
Year of Faith

On a hot August Sunday in 1899, D. L. Moody preached to a New York City audience:

Someday, you will read in the papers that Moody . . . is dead. Don't believe a word of it! At that moment I shall be more alive than I am now. . . . I was born of the flesh in 1837. I was born of the Spirit in 1856. That which is born of the flesh may die. That which is born of the Spirit will live forever.[1]

Moody's life epitomized faith.

Little did Moody realize that by December 22, he would be dead. In April of 1899, he spoke with power to the Chicago Avenue Church, which he founded. On that occasion, he reminded his audience that after thirty-five years his message was unchanged. "Human nature has not changed in the last 1,900 years. Should I preach a different gospel from that which was successful in apostolic days? Oh, bosh!"

He continued, "What can save the life of a nation? Only the strength of an awakened church, and the church can only be awakened by a visitation of power such as the apostles received." Then he added with a chuckle, "If my theology isn't the same now as I preached thirty years ago, I would bundle it up, drop it into the Mississippi, and let it float down to the Gulf of Mexico."

A few months later, Moody led another successful summer conference at Northfield, Massachusetts. His spirit remained strong even in the throes of personal tragedy. In November 1898, his one-year-old grandson (his namesake) died. Nine months later, his five-year-old granddaughter, Irene, passed away. Tenderly, Moody spoke of her:

> She was very fond of riding with me, and Monday morning, twenty-four hours before she fell asleep, she asked me to take her driving. . . . She never looked more beautiful. She was ripening for heaven. She was too fair for this earth. I thank God this morning for the hope of immortality. I know I shall see her more beautiful in her resplendent glory than she was here.[2]

Moody spent much of September 1899 in Chicago at his beloved school. Some close friends observed that he lacked his usual vigor. Shortly before addressing the students, he complained of faintness and, at the last minute, asked Dr. James M. Gray to speak for him.

Again in early November, on his way to what proved to be his last preaching series, at the Kansas City Convention Hall, he visited his Chicago Bible Institute for the last time. "He stood before the students in the lecture room," his son Will wrote later, "and as he closed, resting one hand on the desk and using the other for slight gestures, the tears running down his cheeks, he said, 'I need power! Pray for me that I may have the power of the Holy Spirit!'"

The Kansas City Convention Hall, seating more than fifteen thousand people, was filled to overflowing twice on the opening Sunday. Moody preached with typical warmth and spirit.

Monday evening, he slept poorly, though he attempted to hide his pain from fellow workers. His soloist observed that he looked pale and ate very little. After the Thursday night sermon, Moody was dripping with sweat and even appeared delirious. It was then, under doctor's orders, that he called to Chicago for R. A. Torrey to come and finish the campaign.

After arriving in Northfield, he telegraphed his Kansas City friends: "Have reached home safely . . . regret exceedingly being forced to leave . . . my prayer is that many will be led into the kingdom under Mr. Torrey's preaching."[3]

Thursday, December 21, he told his family, "I'm not discouraged. I want to live as long as I am useful, but when my work is done I want to be up and off."

The next day, Moody awakened after a restless night. In careful, measured words he said, "Earth recedes, Heaven opens for me!" His son, Will, concluded his father was dreaming. "No, this is no dream, Will. It is beautiful. It is like a trance. If this is death, it is sweet.

There is no valley here. God is calling me, and I must go."[4]

Shortly after, he added, "This is my triumph; this is my coronation day!"[5] After speaking these words, he quietly slipped into God's presence.

Death was sweet for D. L. Moody because his doubts were met by faith.

NOTES

1. "The Autobiography of Dwight L. Moody." William R. Moody, *The Life of Dwight L. Moody* (New York: Revell, 1900), frontispiece and 554–55.
2. Ibid., 541.
3. Ibid., 549.
4. Ibid., 552.
5. Ibid., 552–53.

But Some Doubted

Believing is tough . . . when your dreams fall apart. That's what the disciples of Jesus faced. They believed enough to worship Him, "but some doubted" (Matthew 28:17). They still had lots of questions.

When Jesus told them plainly that He would "go to Jerusalem, and suffer . . . and be killed, and be raised again the third day" (Matthew 16:21), it killed their dream. Peter bluntly scolded Jesus, and told Him to forget it (v. 22).

A short time later, while Jesus sat with His twelve disciples, in what is called "The Last Supper," He warned, "You will have tribulation, but be of good cheer, I have overcome the world" (John 16:33). Upon hearing that, their faith temporarily revived. Shocking as it seems, by the next day, all eleven disciples turned and fled (Matthew 26:56). What Jesus had revealed in the light was forgotten . . . in the dark.

When Jesus was in the Garden of Gethsemane, He too faced indescribable anguish. "O My Father, . . . let this cup pass from Me; nevertheless, not as I will, but as You will" (Matthew 26:39). Jesus questioned, "Is there any other way than this?" And yet, He was willing to suffer . . . if God willed it. And later, while dying on the cross, He called out, "Why have You forsaken me?" (27:46). The suffering of Jesus tells the whole world once and forever how God feels about pain. God cares about human suffering.

Following Jesus' death, the disciples were disillusioned. They had huge *doubts*. Two of His followers, three days later, while walking the road to Emmaus, confessed, "*we were hoping* that it was He who was going to redeem Israel"; however, "today is the third day since these things happened" (Luke 24:21, emphasis added).

"They had good chronology, and good theology, but no doxology," said Vance Havner. They were in the doldrums of doubt. While these two followers were in this state of confusion . . . the resurrected Jesus revealed Himself to them and their doubts were forever banished. They rushed to tell the other disciples, the good news (see vv. 33–34).

Because of the compassion of Jesus, no one ever needs to ask, "Does God care?" Suffering does not mean that God has forsaken us. Jesus sat where . . . we sit! Through His life on earth, He experienced every conceivable pain that comes to us. "We do not have a High Priest who cannot sympathize with our weaknesses, *but was in all points* tempted as we are, yet without sin" (Hebrews 4:15, emphasis added).

It's life changing to view the doubts of Good Friday in the light and victory of Easter Sunday.

Don't doubt in the dark . . . what God has revealed in the light.

50

Anchors to Hold

It has been said, "You know you're getting older when you bend down to tie your shoelaces and think, 'Is there anything else I ought to do while I'm down here?'"

The body as well as everything else that is seen . . . is dying. Flowers fade . . . leaves fall . . . skin wrinkles . . . and bodies bend. Paul expresses this condition in these words, "The things which are seen are temporary, but the things which are not seen are eternal" (2 Corinthians 4:18).

Even civilizations, as great as they may be, rise, rule for a time, and eventually rot. Seen things do not last, while unseen certainties . . . last forever.

Paul shares three anchors to live and die by. The first anchor is *the certainty of a future resurrection*. Paul was positive of this "unseen certainty." "Knowing that He who raised up the Lord Jesus will also raise us up with Jesus" (2 Corinthians 4:14).

Evangelist D. L. Moody said, "Someday you will read in the papers that Moody . . . is dead. Don't you believe a word of it! At that moment I shall be more alive than I am now. . . . I was born of the flesh in 1837, I was born of the Spirit in 1855. That which is born of the flesh may die. That which is born of the Spirit will live forever."[1]

Apart from the certainty of the Resurrection, life would be unbearable. Paul puts it this way: "If Christ is not risen, your faith is futile" (1 Corinthians 15:17). "If in this life only we have hope in Christ, we are of all men the most pitiable" (v. 19). Paul wagered his life on the "certainty of the resurrection."

The second anchor is an "eternal weight of glory" (2 Corinthians 4:17). Paul contrasts human afflictions, which are relatively short-lived here on earth, with eternal, unbounded, abundant, heavenly treasures. Seventy years of life may seem long . . . but contrasted to eternity in God's presence, it's like—as Teresa of Avila put it—"one bad night in an inconvenient hotel."[2] "These troubles and sufferings of ours are, after all, quite small and won't last very long" (2 Corinthians 4:17 TLB). It is life changing to view each day with eternity in mind.

The third anchor is "a house not made with hands, eternal in the heavens" (2 Corinthians 5:1). Faith in a future eternal home, though unseen, is an anchor that is secure in the storms of life.

Our earthly bodies are frail at best. Scripture likens the human body to an "earthen vessel" (see 2 Corinthians 4:7), literally, a clay pot, which is easily fractured and broken. In another place, the human body is compared to "a tent" that is so flimsy that it needs only to be struck by a barley cake and it will collapse (Judges 7:13). These bodies of ours will one day perish, but we have "a house not made with hands, eternal in the heavens" (2 Corinthians 5:1). The hymn writer has written:

> Someday my earthly house will fall,
> I cannot tell how soon 'twill be.
> But this I know—my All in All
> Has now a place in heav'n for me.[3]

Here are three anchors of the soul that are guaranteed to banish doubt and build faith.

With Paul we can exult, "Thanks be to God, who gives us the victory through our Lord Jesus Christ" (1 Corinthians 15:57). Because of these certainties, I can confidently say: Don't doubt in the dark . . . what God has revealed in the light.

NOTES

1. "The Autobiography of Dwight L. Moody." William R. Moody, *The Life of Dwight L. Moody* (New York: Revell, 1900), frontispiece and 554–55.
2. Peter Kreeft, *Making Sense of Suffering* (Ann Arbor, Mich.: Servant, 1986), 139.
3. Fanny Crosby (1820–1915), "Saved by Grace."

Too Soon to Quit

No matter what the season or circumstances of your life, you can prosper and actually grow stronger! This book urges you to press on in the power and strength of Jesus, the ultimate example of *not* quitting. Each page bolsters your resolve, lights your path, and deepens your faith. 0-8024-8329-1

MOODY
The Name You Can Trust

George Sweeting

How to Begin the Christian Life

REVISED

How to Begin the Christian Life

This modern classic which has helped thousands get a strong start in their Christian lives can do the same for you. Few men are better equipped than George Sweeting to explain how to begin the most excellent adventure of your life. 0-8024-3581-5

MOODY
The Name You Can Trust